Show Me,

Teach Me,

Heal Me

Show Me, Teach Me, Heal Me

A Beginner's Guide to Natural Answers

Acaysha Dolfin
and Six Spiritual Friends

TRAFFORD

 www.trafford.com

North America & international
toll-free: 1 888 232 4444 (USA & Canada)
phone: 250 383 6864 ♦ fax: 812 355 4082

Dedication

I would like to dedicate this book to a very special lady, Beverly Toney Walter. An angel in disguise, who saw me for whom I could become and helped me discover my true potential and purpose in life. Without her faith in me at a time when I needed guidance, I would not be here today writing my second book. THANKS BEV for believing in me so strongly !!

I would like to also thank Dr. Hirschorn and Dr. Zimmerman of the Scottsdale Mayo Clinic, my neurologist, and neurosurgeon, respectively, for making this new life and dream possible !! Thank you for giving me a chance at a better life, one with a purpose and true meaning. You both are truly angels in disguise – thank you for touching my life !!

Many Thanks

I would also like to thank each of the authors who donated their time and energy in contributing a chapter to this book with their love and knowledge - Rebecca Blair, Brian Dean, Rev. Karen Wilkinson, Lanis Loveday Chidel, Rosann Lynch, and Susanne Murphy. Without you all and your wonderful informative chapters this book would not be have come to be – THANK YOU – May we all benefit from the success of this book and everything you do in this lifetime!!

Many people have touched my life along my path in the thirty-seven years that I have been searching for answers to my own health problems and concerns. Thanks to each of you who asked along the way, "How's the book coming, how is your health, have you found an answer to your health concern?" Your interest and support has made this creation not only mine, but ours ! Thanks for helping to keep me focused on the end result and finishing this project so I can share it with the world. To all of my friends, too numerous to mention, for their unconditional love and support along this journey.

Also thanks to all of my spiritual teachers and healers who have come into my life and enriched it for the better. Thanks for all of the healings, guidance and teachings, I have received, I couldn't have done it without you !!

A special thank you to my book designer MyLinda Butterworth and my editor Patricia Behnke, without their expertise, this book would never have come to be.

Foreword

In the past two years, I have faced more tragic events than some people face in an entire lifetime. The mechanisms I used the first 46 years of my life suddenly failed me, and I found myself unable to cope with my own losses. For an entire year, I was able to be strong for everyone around me, all the while hiding the fact that I was hanging on by a thread.

The thread broke last year, and I have been searching for hope once again in my life. On one of my journeys, I met Acaysha and her angels. Somehow, I decided to travel five hours from my home to a book signing that Acaysha had arranged. I only knew her through the Internet and our writer's group, and I knew nothing about the book signing she had arranged. However, I went and within an hour I knew what had brought me.

When she needed someone to help in the editing of this book, I said I would do it. However much I may have helped her, the reading of this book and its lessons has brought me far more. Despair still overcomes me at times as I continue to clean up the messes left from the storms of the past two years, but with the guidance of the Divine Spirit, I have come to find peace and release in the advice found within the pages of *Show Me Teach Me Heal Me, A Beginner's Guide to Natural Answers*.

After going through all the help that could be offered in the "traditional" ways, the discovery of self became lost and perhaps delayed my true healing. What I find most compelling about this book is the message that we choose the life we live. We make decisions daily that can impact our life for the better; if that is the path we have chosen.

I hope the readers of this book will also find peace in the course of healing pain, either physical or emotional, and with that knowledge spread hope to others who have lost their faith.

Patricia C. Behnke, Author
A Victorian Justice and A Lethal Legacy
October 2003
High Springs, Florida

Who is Acaysha?

Someone who is caring, forgiving, kind, thoughtful, generous,
special, angelic and a true friend
Someone who has beaten the odds and was reborn
Someone who accepted challenges with dignity and grace
Someone who walks on faith
Someone who has taught me to take risks
someone who lives life to the fullest
Someone who touches the lives of many
All of these things describe - - - Acaysha.

Many blessings,
Rev. Karen Wilkinson

Table of Contents

Chapter One

Introduction

how Me, Teach Me, Heal Me, a Beginner's Guide to Natural Answers, was written to help you get control of your life and your health, and to give you new and natural answers to health problems and concerns, to teach you that your health is your responsibility, not your parents, spouses, or doctors!! In our society we have been raised to believe that our health depends on the quality of the healthcare we receive, and that our doctors always know what is best. The truth is, your health is your responsibility. You are the only person who can make the lifestyle decisions that contribute to your well-being and with this book, we want to give you the tools to start making those educated decisions. You are the one who must take the steps to preserve your health and promote your wellness. Isn't it wonderful to be back in charge of your own health? Scary too, I know. I was there once, but with good guidance, great teachers and some faith, I made it through and started making educated decisions that have improved my life dramatically!

My name is Acaysha Dolfin and this is the second book I have written. My first book *NEW HORIZONS AND MY ANGELS*, is about my journey through brain surgery recovery, after having surgery to stop my epileptic seizures and starting living my life to the fullest. Along the path, I became very allergic to most traditional medicines and techniques, surprising after having medication pushed down me for over 20 years. I was forced to go natural and holistic, if I wanted to get my health back and improve the quality of life I was hoping to have. So along the way, I learned about several techniques that could help improve my health and mental attitude, and they are included in this book. About two years into my recovery stage I was given seven angels to guide me, teach me, and show me how to live my life to the fullest, learning to laugh and love the process we call life. They taught me how to make the right decisions, which would impact my life for the better. I had been asking for guidance, answers, teachers, healers to help me get well so I could be done with healing process, and then I had seven of them, and they are still in my life today !! I am very blessed and very grateful, but you too can have a band of angels to teach and guide you. Check out the chapter on angels in this book or listen to my meditation CDs on how to connect with your angels!

Having brain surgery was the hardest, most challenging, exciting, invigorating and frustrating thing I have ever undertaken in this lifetime, but now in 2003, I am 11 years seizure free and living my dreams – it was worth it!! Thank you, Dr. Zimmerman and Dr. Hirschorn, for believing in me and giving me a chance at a better life!!

The biggest lesson I had to learn was that only I had the power to create wellness for myself, not anyone else — no pills, no doctors, no family could do it for me — just me!! This power lies within and in the decisions and choices we make every day. If you choose to react out of habit or fixed attitudes, you will get the same results you always have, which may not be in the best interest of your health and well-being. To create wellness both inside and out, you must expand your understandings beyond just your physical ailments and symptoms, drugs, surgeries and quick fixes; and start striving to balance all aspects of your life and take an active role in your health decisions and healing process.

Our society is overwhelmed by an excess of materialism and vertiginous pace, which cause feelings of fragmentation, confusion and pressure throughout our lives, both in our personal relationships and at work. Many people end up expressing their unbalanced condition through illness, sometimes severe, and then find conventional medicine limited to solve their problems. The Philosophy of *Show Me Teach Me Heal Me, a Beginner's Guide to Natural Answers* is based upon the concept of the human being as a whole. From that whole vision, we believe that the human being has the capacity to transform, grow, and cure itself, once one gets the means to really connect with themselves, with their inner being. This book offers a different approach, to help to alleviate ill health through treating the person as a whole combining all levels of being, physical, emotional, psychological and energetic.

So I am writing this book along with some wonderful spiritual friends of mine to help answer some of your hardest questions, like where do I start, what is it about, how do I know what to do, what are my friends talking about, will it hurt me, what other options do I have, the doctors are giving up on me now what, how do I find someone to help me along my path to getting well....

To understand wellness, you need to view your all parts of your body, and view each as a separate, but integral part of you to help make you a whole and complete person.

- ௯ **The Physical body** - this is your body, which encompasses your five senses: touch, see, hear, smell and taste.

- ௯ **The Emotional body** – this is your emotional side of you, with feelings ranging from fear and anger to love and joy and everything in-between.

- ௯ **The Mental body** – this is your thoughts, attitudes, and beliefs in life. This is what helps make up your personality.

- ௯ **The Spiritual body** - this is part of you that deals with your creativity, your life purpose, and your relationship with a Higher Power.

This relationship between the different parts of you is referred to as the mind/body connection. In this book, you will learn many ways how your physical, mental, emotional, and spiritual bodies are connected and how each one impacts the other. They have to work in harmony to achieve total health and well-being and when any part of your body is out of balance, it will let you know. Your attentiveness can help you maintain a total balance and achieve perfect health.

ଓ Your **physical** body requires good nutrition, appropriate
weight, beneficial exercise and adequate rest. Learn to listen to
your body — what makes it feel good and what makes it hurt.
Are you getting heartburn, upset stomach, diarrhea — maybe
your body is trying to tell you that it doesn't like the food you
just gave it, or you are allergic to it. Try eliminating those foods
and see if the symptoms go away, instead of just taking a pill to
fix the problem. Are you eating healthy fresh foods, avoiding
excessive sugars and fats, or are you going through the drive-
thrus of life? Do you drink water everyday, or is it just coffee,
sodas, and alcohol? Your body needs water to re-hydrate your
skin, your organs, and muscles, and without it you will develop
health conditions. Do you exercise your body in some way, or
are you a couch or computer potato? It has been proven we
need to physically move our bodies for 20 minutes three times
a week to keep it healthy and physically charged. Are you getting enough sleep, or are those bags under your eyes perma-
nent? Those too are a sign of lack of sleep and food allergies.
Everyone's body has a natural rhythm to it and finding yours
and how much sleep your body needs is a trial and error ex-
periment you get to perform.

ଓ Your **emotional** body needs to laugh, love, play and feel to
stay balanced. Hiding your emotions from yourself or others
will not contribute to a total well-being. Learn to watch your
reactions to certain people, activities or events. How do they
make you feel? All feelings are valid, so allow yourself to feel!
Sometimes just taking time out to play, be silly, and do child-
like activities, is one of the best prescriptions you can take. By
taking time out to play and laugh, you will stay younger, feel
more alive and enjoy all aspects of your life more. You are a
valuable part of this universe; you have meaning and purpose.
Sharing your gifts and talent with others enhances both of our
lives. By sharing yourself, you can help someone else in their
own life; you can be their angel, even if only for a moment or a
season.

ଓ Your **mental** body needs positive thoughts, inspiring viewpoints,
and a positive self-image. How you were raised can impact

how you view yourself and your net worth, but you are still the pilot of your own life. You can change how you view yourself and others through visualization, meditation and thought. Try exploring some new ideas. Find a hobby, read a good book, take an educational class, volunteer, and help someone less fortunate than you. Some people turn their hobbies into a passion or a business. Try something new; you just might like it!! Attitudes are contagious — is yours worth catching? Is the glass half full or half empty? It is all in the eyes of the beholder. Try finding something to smile about, even watch a butterfly. Smiling is contagious....catch it !! Check your beliefs. Are they working for you now? They may have worked for you when you were a kid. Are they working for you now. If not, change them. You are responsible for your own happiness.

cs Your **spiritual** body requires inner peace, serenity and calmness. It is your connection to your gut feeling or inner knowing of something. Intuition is something we all have. Are you using yours to guide you, to be creative and to help you create the life you want? Take time to meditate, pray, or just have quiet time with yourself. We each need to get in touch with our inner selves, either through a higher power, our angels or any way that works for us. There is no right or wrong way, but by doing it, you will find your purpose, your passions and your real life dreams.

As you become aware of your physical, emotional, mental and spiritual condition you can act quickly to prevent illness and disease, if one is out balance. You will learn a lot in this book and see how many different opportunities you have to embrace your health and well-being. This is your life and there are no dress rehearsals!! No one's life is perfect, as much as the fairy tales and TV shows make us think they are. We all have illnesses, hard situations, difficult times, and losses to deal with. Have you noticed some people seem to handle their lives and situations better than others? Have you ever wondered why? A lot has to do with attitude! Are you just accepting anything and everything that is thrown at you feeling like the victim, or are you taking an active role in your life and how YOU control it? Being in the victim seat will leave you feeling helpless, hopeless, and depressed. Is that really where you want to be?

Achieving wellness is an on-going series of small steps, taken one day at a time, so "enjoy the journey," as my angels would say !! Since wellness is not going to happen overnight, please make a commitment to yourself to continue to discover the most appropriate methods for you and your total well-being. This book will help guide you down the path to health and well-being and teach you how to choose natural answers for your life. Enjoy!! If I can help you in any way or you would like to come to one of my holistic centers in the United States, please don't hesitate to call me, or anyone else listed in this book. We are here to help you along the your path!!

So starting now – you are going to take an active role in your life, your health and your total well-being!! One step forward, no matter how small or slow is a movement in the right direction. You are now an active participant and one step closer to total health and well-being. You are a WINNER!

Acaysha

Chapter Two

Angels and How They Impact Our Lives Today

A ngels are an obvious reality of religious history and of biblical study. Angels are no myth. They are a very evident and a significant part of history and spirituality. The word angel comes from the Greek angelos, which means messenger. The word is applied to both human and divine messengers, especially the god Hermes in Greek mythology. Angels are around us every day, waiting to help us, guide us, and show us the way to a better and more fulfilling life. There are several references of angels in the Bible, as they go as far back in history as we can search. They are still evident and active in our lives today.

Here is an excerpt from my first book *NEW HORIZONS AND MY ANGELS*, which is my personal story of how I became aware that I had angels in my world.

"Earlier that year (1995), I was working on my computer, putting a newsletter together for my team players, when all of a sudden I saw a glimpse of a bright light in the room. I was startled and kind of scared. I looked around to see if anyone was there, but I saw no one. Being religious and feeling close to God, I quickly yelled out, "Who are you and what do you want? If you are good, you can stay, and if not then get the heck out of here, NOW!!"

I stood there waiting for something to happen and nothing did. So I returned to my computer and tried to continue working. Whoever or

whatever this bright light was, decided to play with me and turn my com-
puter off, right before my eyes!! I was stunned and a bit upset because
they forgot to save my work. I yelled again "Who are you and what do you
*want?? **and still no answer.***

I decided I needed a break, so I left the computer off and went into my
bedroom to pray and meditate. I asked God what was going on and who
or what was this "being" and did they mean any harm to me. After sitting
there quietly for a while, which felt like eternity, I finally got an answer. I
heard a voice say….

"We are angels and we are sent here by God to help you. We are going
to teach you a lot about life, living, growing up, and loving. There are seven
of us and we mean no harm to you."

I was quickly relieved, but still a bit hesitant. I then fell asleep into a
deep meditative state and felt much better upon rising. I returned to my
computer work with a new energy and passion. All of a sudden, I felt like
I wasn't so alone anymore, and that maybe God was really listening to all
my prayers!! I had been asking for guidance, answers, teachers, healers,
*etc., to help me get well so I could be done with this recovery process. **Now***
I had seven of them! THANK YOU, GOD!!

During my quiet times, the angels would speak to me, mainly through
my artwork, as they taught me how to paint on T-shirts. I would surrender
to them late at night and allow them, while I was in meditation, to teach
me to draw and paint, something I didn't know I could do. Each morning
I would wake up and run into the dining room, where I had been laying
the night before, to see what I had created. I was always in amazement!!
I learned to laugh that year, something I had forgotten how to do. Being
so depressed, yet intensely determined to get well, I had not lightened up
on myself at all. I had forgotten the rule that you have to laugh at yourself
or you will cry!

Even my newsletter and articles of inspiration for my team players
changed that year. My team grew in leaps and bounds and everyone was
growing stronger in their own businesses. I had grown in my business, not
only as a strong manager and leader, but also as a glamour make-up art-
ist and I was loving it. I was one of the fastest make-up artists on the West
Coast!! So I got to keep my wandering spirit happy by being able to travel
to salons all over California and do glamour shots for women. Not only

was I making money and loving it, I was recruiting up a storm, which was needed for me to succeed to the next level.

Moving to Monterey in 1996 one of my neatest and most rewarding moves in this lifetime. The angels were right there every step of the way, guiding me, teaching me, laughing and crying with me. In February 1996, I finally got to "see" my angels, and they were really beautiful... all seven of them !! They were small in size, but very angelic and graceful looking. They looked a lot like what people call "cherubs" today. They came to me in a dream and told me I was going to start designing clothes for a living! I almost laughed, as I didn't like to sew, and wasn't a professional artist either! I didn't really believe in my artistic talent and could not see this happening at all. So I asked for some confirmation from them and over the next seven days, I had total strangers tell me the outfits that I had made and wore were gorgeous and asked me what boutique I bought them!! On the seventh day, my angels came to me and said, "Well do you believe us now?" I agreed. So with them by my side, guiding me every step of the way, I started my own clothing company called T_he Added Touch – Clothing with Added Flair._ I was willing to learn and with this team of seven angels, I was willing to try anything!!

*During this season, the angels finally let me paint them so others could see them, too. Boy were they beautiful! As I sat at the computer trying to come up with traditional angel names for them, I heard one angel say, "That's not my name!" I was shocked, but since I was more comfortable with them, I replied, "Oh, so what is your name?" I was expecting any one of many names, but not the one she typed. She erased what I had typed and typed, "Child's Play." I was stunned and I said, "That is not an angel name," for which she quickly responded, "OK, but that is my name!!" She said she was here to **teach me to laugh, cry, and play – just like a kid and to learn to love my "inner child."** She was my "three-year old child." Boy, was I in for a lot of great adventures with her. She was the most outspoken of them all, and the funniest. She would make me do crazy things like eat a candy bar, put my feet in the sand at the beach, and ride with the windows down (when it was 50 degrees outside!!) — crazy, but fun-spirited things! I learned to live again through her. She helped me give names to all the other angels too, none of them like I would have named them.*

Here's a poem I wrote:

Life's Twists and Turns

*Life is full of twists and turns; no one said it was going to
    be easy, straight and narrow with no bends, bumps or
    curves in the road.*

*Life really is one lifelong "test" of one's faith; how much
    you believe, how much you withstand, how far you
    bend, and finding your breaking point.*

*Everyone's breaking point is at a different level and only
    God really knows where it is, as He / She is always
    pushing on it and pushing it higher and higher.*

*The tough times can be very trying, stressful and emotion-
    ally draining, but when the experience is over you are
    wiser and stronger and with more faith than before.*

*Life really is just a series of short plays, each with a differ-
    ent set of actors or actresses, each with a new and differ-
    ent theme and outcome each and every time.*

*So stop taking life so seriously and learn to enjoy the ride.
    Realize you are the star of your own play, so lighten up,
    laugh more and live it to the fullest.*

*Life is definitely a play, except there are no rehearsals, as
    it changes every day. When one gets too lax or comfort-
    able, life delivers a new challenge to unpack.*

*Unfortunately, most challenges don't come with instruction
    manuals or guides!*

*When one thinks life is so bad with no hope for the future,
    God will bring in an angel to lift you up and give you
    new energy and hope.*

*Sometimes these angels will stay a long time; others will dis-
    appear in the middle of the night. Some will back off to
    give you space to grow and experience new things.*

*They move far enough away that you miss them more, but
    are still close enough for you to know they are near.*

*Absence makes the heart grow fonder and truer, and you
    learn to appreciate those in your life more.*

Child's Play is still very active in my life today and I love it!! Actually all seven angels are still in my life today, and are continuously helping me grow, learn and enjoy life to the fullest. You too can have your own band of angels to help you live your life to the fullest; hopefully this chapter and my audio CD collection titled *Field of Angels*, *Swim With The Dolphins* and *Angels in the Rainbows* will help you find yours! I plan to share my newfound wisdom and life experiences with the general public as my wonderful team of angels continue to teach me new ways of living, loving and laughing.

My angels have taught me so much about life, love, and laughter, and how to really enjoy the journey we all call "life," and now I am being guided to share that knowledge with you!!

GUARDIAN ANGELS

Guardian angels are 100 percent committed to you for your entire life here on earth. Angels will not intrude on your free will, but they can guide you, teach you, and love you unconditionally. They are individual companions and protectors for ONE human being. They support us in fulfilling our own life's plan. Each of us has our own guardian angel, who has been protecting and guiding us from birth. It is fairly common for people to first come in contact with their guardian angel during a dangerous situation when they are somehow saved or rescued.

ARCHANGELS

MICHAEL: Michael battles evil, challenges people who have evil or negative intentions and helps people open up to new ways of thinking, bringing courage for spiritual experiences. He is the guardian of divine order and accompanies human beings on their path between the poles of duality. He keeps the path of return open for the soul, no matter how far one has strayed. He grants miracles and fosters mercy, repentance, truth, sanctification, blessing, immortality, patience, and love to humankind.

RAPHAEL: He heals all areas of our being, not just the body, but also the feelings, thoughts, situations and our connection to God, to light and to oneness. He nourishes and strengthens, which makes him responsible for every kind of healing, regeneration, rejuvenation, and renewal on earth. Raphael grants joy, healing, love miracles, and grace.

GABRIEL: He announces God's plans and actions and is most often associated with a trumpet. He brought forth the news of Jesus to Mary (Luke 1:26-38) and the birth of John to Zacharias. Gabriel brings divine consciousness, such as joy, ecstasy, liveliness, and dance to earth. He encourages us to dance with life and is especially effective in times of difficulty, depression, and hopelessness.

URIEL: As the archangel of prophecy and transformation, Uriel helps us complete goals and life missions. He brings us into the here and now, carries consciousness into the ordinary world and helps us live our spirituality in everyday life.

HANIEL: Haniel watches over beauty, love, happiness, pleasure and harmony. His energy uplifts us, reminds us of who we really are, which abilities we have, and gives us courage to live these qualities. Haniel inspires mortals to love in a grounded way, guiding us to always remain in harmony with our deepest spiritual wisdom.

RAZIEL: Archangel of mysteries, Raziel questions mysteries one might encounter while on their spiritual journey. Raziel inspires us to dig deeper in search of divine knowledge and truth.

CHAMUEL: Angel of charity and tolerance, he brings divine beauty to earth and inspires all of artistic activities. He is responsible for harmonizing all types of relationships: relationship with ourselves, with others, with nature, and with God. Chamuel helps us to drop judgmental attitudes toward others and develop a more tolerant view of our own shortcomings.

ZADKIEL: Angel of growth, development, and completion, Zadkiel develops the highest potential of every being: the perfect form, the perfect nature, and the perfect structure. He connects people with their potential and with their divine aspect and perfect being.

An excerpt from the book *God Invented Angels First* explains best what angels look like:

God invented angels before He made everything else.
Angels are God's helpers and messengers.
They tell people what God wants them to know.
There are all kinds of angels
BIG angels, LITTLE angels, BOY angels, GIRL angels.
And some angels you don't know what they are.
Some angels have wings, some don't have wings.
Some wings are VERY BIG, some are teeny tiny.
All angels have halo light around them.
This is their energy showing and it is very beautiful
Angels have names.
Some have important-sounding fancy names,
Some have names like yours.
Ask your angel what its name is. Your angel will tell you.
Yes, you can talk to your angel.
It is very easy to chat with an angel.
Angels are always with you to listen and visit with you.
Angels even will talk back to you.

We are just spiritual beings having a physical experience this lifetime and when our earthwork is done, we will pass over to the other side and join the many angels above and help those still on earth. We become a form of pure and unconditional love; anything less than pure love is not an angel.

Angels have the most universal knowledge and broadest prospective on all matters. Angels are teachers, sent here to help guide us and give us a clearer perspective on the larger picture of life. Angels do a lot of things, but they will not take away your free will or the lesson you are here on earth to learn. They don't judge, scold, preach, or give advice you don't ask for.

WHAT DO ANGELS DO?

Angels Do God's Work
 Angels Love
  Angels Teach
   Angels Comfort
    Angels Support
     Angels Protect
      Angels do God's work.
       We do what God tells us to do.
    We bring you what is best and what God decides.
            That is all.

PREPARATION TO MEET OUR ANGELS

Set up a place where you can retreat without being disturbed. Somewhere out in nature or a quiet room in the house.

Sit or lay down comfortably.

Close your eyes and breathe deeply. Imagine you are lying in a meadow. Feel the ground beneath your back and the grass that gently touches your arms and legs. You can see the blue sky and fluffy white clouds. The birds are singing and the flowers are in full bloom, gently swaying in the wind. The air is filled with a pleasant fragrance of blossoms. Feel your whole body unwinding and relaxing quietly into the meadow and the moment. Invite the sunrays to penetrate your body and envelop you in a beautiful iridescent bubble of glowing warm light. As you let it move through every organ and cell in your body, ask it to release any blockages that no longer serve you; ask it to release what doesn't belong to you or prevents you from living your life to the fullest; ask it to send them back to the universe, as you no longer need them. Ask that they dissolve those blockages away, to make you aware of the change in your body, now and later. Let all your thoughts and worries just float away and go higher and higher into the clouds. As you feel yourself letting everything go, allow your mind to wander and ask for your angels to come and speak with you. Then lie quietly and just breathe. They will appear and speak quietly. If it is too softly for you, nicely ask them to speak louder. Allow them to teach you, guide you, and heal you, as they only work for your highest good. Surrender your problems and concerns to them, give them everything including your wishes, dreams, hopes, difficulties, old matters, pain — EVERY-THING!

They will do their part in helping you in your life, and then they will guide you on what you need to do. ASK ANYTHING – the more you learn to include them in your life, the stronger your connection will be and the clearer your perception will be, too. When done talking with them, thank them for their guidance and divine wisdom.

ASKING FOR SPIRITUAL HELP

1. Before going to sleep, meditate for fifteen minutes and ask your personal guides or angels to help you with your problem while you are sleeping.
2. You may want to speak these words aloud, "I ask my Guides and Angels to help me solve the problem of _____. I ask that I meet up with these Higher Beings in my dreams tonight to discuss the matter fully. I will listen to their divine answers and advice. In the morning I will remember the dream and conversation and then decide with my own best judgment, how to act upon the problem."
3. Protect yourself spiritually in a golden/white light, shaped like an auric egg or bubble. Surround yourself and go to sleep.
4. In the morning when you wake, immediately write down, in your dream journal, any conversations you have had or thoughts that come to you.
5. If the advice seems right for you, act upon it!

Your Angels are there in the Higher Dimensions to guide you on your journey through life. They are not there to command you to do anything, as they value your free will!

So it is essential, that you always try to manifest conditions and things from the Highest Intent (to help yourself and others in a positive way) and from Unconditional Love (so you don't hurt anyone in the process).

If you remember to put in these sensible provisions, then your desire to manifest will always be honorable. Faith is an important issue in the manifestation process. If you don't really believe that it will happen, you are unconsciously squashing the deal! So always be positive.

Also, don't overly attach to the object you desire, making sure you can live without it, if you have to. Then you are creating the right atmosphere to attain your goal. Allow the Universe to send your desired object or situation, in a free flowing, timeless manner. In other words, don't hassle the Universe. Do your part in trying to gently achieve your goal, but don't force the issue. Tell the Universe what you desire, but don't demand it!

FOUR (4) FUNDAMENTAL STEPS TO SUCCESSFUL LIVING

Ask: Be specific and focus on what you really want. Clarity is the key to formulating what you would like to have. Remember the saying "be careful what you ask for, you just might get it." The law of free will says that angels cannot intervene in our lives without our express permission. BE VERY SPECIFIC WHAT YOU WANT. Angels are empowered to bring you help in every area of your life. Don't ask for a tent when you really want a house! Asking involves expectancy. BE SPECIFIC AND ASK BIG!!

Believe: After you have asked for what you would like to come into your life, your next step is to BELIEVE and TRUST that it is the right thing for you, with the caveat that it is part of your divine plan for being here. If it is, then it will happen. Allow the angels to work for your greatest good and believe they will bring it to you. Believing involves TRUST — don't be afraid. God and the Angels never ask you to change or move forward without a support system around you. Surrender the problem completely and believe they are working for you.

Let It Happen: This step requires PATIENCE, and human patience is not very deep. The temptation to control things instead of just letting it happen is the HARDEST STEP! Letting go is allowing the angels to work on your wishes, and it is proof that YOU BELIEVE. You do not need to repeat, worry, or beg — it is like letting bread rise, the more you play with it, the less it will happen. SO JUST LET IT BE! Expect positive results and it will happen. Allow what you have asked come to you and believe you will receive it. Be open, receptive and patient so you don't get in the way. It will come in DIVINE TIME. "Let Go and Let God" is the best advice out there so that God can let it go to you!

Thank You: Remember to give thanks once you have received what you requested. This step completes the circle and reinforces the third step, letting it happen. This method will empower you. These four steps are positive fundamentals for spiritual living, and they teach you it is OK to ask. If you cannot ask your angels for what you need and desire, then how can you ask your boss for a raise?

When you use these fundamental rules, you will notice immediate changes in your life. People will begin to see your changes in beauty, happiness, and peace; fear and loneliness will disappear. Your life will work better; joy, peace and success will be yours!

How do you learn these skills?

PRACTICE, PRACTICE, PRACTICE!!!!

Pray for guidance and insight. Remain open to the skill and allow it come to you. Remember all knowledge is already within you; you just need to learn how to access it. Skills come from practice and repetition and knowledge comes in many ways, such as study, dreams, and experiences.

The importance of the Four (4) Fundamentals in your life cannot be overstated!!
ASK AND YOU WILL RECEIVE!!

TO CONNECT WITH YOUR ANGELS IN WRITING, ALL YOU NEED TO DO IS: PRAY, BREATHE, LISTEN, WRITE, ACCEPT, FOLLOW YOUR INNER KNOWING, AND TRUST

Step 1: <u>PRAY</u>

Ask to be a clear channel and keep yourself and ego out of it. Pray for the truth and the gift of spiritual healing. It does not matter how you pray; it is the intention that starts the energy flow process.

Step 2: <u>BREATHE</u>

Sit and relax, concentrate on your breathing, allow yourself to breath slow, long, deep breaths, but don't force it. Allow divine energy and the angel's spirit to come in on your inhale and all stresses and worries leave on the exhale, making more room for the angel's beautiful presence in your life. Breathe now – this is your angel's love you feel.

Step 3: LISTEN

Listen as they come to you as a whisper, it is the same voice that has been guiding you for years. The voice that says, "Go a different way to work" (to avoid an accident), "Turn off the iron" (that you forgot to turn off,) "Call a friend right then (not later) as they need to hear your sweet voice now. Occasionally when you begin to become more aware, you may see colors more intensely, hear more clearly, or feel a strong sense of energy around you. This awareness is normal so do not be afraid. Listening is an attitude of openness and trust.

Step 4: WRITE

Just write — the harder you think, the less flow there will be. Whether it is a few words or a complete sentence, trust the process, and just write what you hear or feel. There is no right or wrong way to receive messages from your angels; you will not be receiving a grade or report card! The key is to BEGIN and just WRITE — trust the process!!

Step 5: ACCEPT

Acceptance is the most important part of the process. You may feel like you made this up, but you didn't. Nothing less than an angel or divine being could communicate with you in this manner. Angels are your most loyal, true-weathered, unconditional love friends you will ever have; they will never steer you wrong.

Step 6: INNER KNOWING

You don't have to think about it or plan it — it just comes!! Angels are totally without ego; they are trustworthy, sometimes silly, but always honest and loving. Receiving messages is like most things in life; the longer you do it, the better and more comfortable with it you become. Inner knowing is a combination of inner peace about the content of the message you receive, and the realization that the angels' communication is loving and supporting and only for your greater and highest good.

Step 7: <u>TRUST</u>

Your angels are asking you for a little bit of time to trust the process of speaking to them. Treat them like your new best friend, give them your time and attention; it will be the BEST GIFT you can ever receive. Listen to your angels: "We are here to help you live, love and laugh more and enjoy the journey you are on and to live it with a passion."

HERE ARE THREE (3) WAYS TO RECEIVE YOUR ANGELIC MESSAGES:
Clairvoyance – the ability to see things not visible to the naked eye. (Second sight)
Clairaudience – the ability to hear sounds not heard by the human ear. (Extended hearing)
Clairsentience – the awareness of knowing beyond the 5 human senses. "Knowing that you know" (and you don't have the foggiest idea HOW you know). (The 6th sense)

IF YOUR EGO OR CONSCIOUS SELF IS MAKING THE PROCESS OF RECEIVING YOUR ANGEL MESSAGES DIFFICULT, WATCH FOR:

A) <u>Doubt:</u>
Stop erasing the angels' message. You received it just fine but then you sit, and dissect it and question it – don't do that! Take it at face value. Don't edit their words either. For example if you hear, "You are kind," don't insert "to most people."
Angels do not give and then take away. They see your great potential where you see your limitations.
B) <u>Poor Reception:</u>
If you don't hear them, first breathe and relax, then ask them to speak louder and more clearly to you. If at first you don't succeed or hear them, try, try again!!
C) <u>Expectations:</u>
What you receive from your angels is the divine truth. It may be a simple or a complex message but either way, trust what they give you and know it is in your best interest to hear them. Angels give you the best they have at that particular moment.

D) Attitudes:

Be positive! Expect goodness and love to come. Ask your angels "please teach me about love that replaces fear, doubt, and worry; please teach me how to have a positive attitude to my life process and replace my ego and negative expectations with joy, peace, and happiness."

Special Note:

Angels can give you guidance, advice, and direction, but you MUST ASK FOR IT. If you ask for help or advice, then you have invited them into your world and are open to their guidance.

☐   If you want to know what vitamin or beauty product to buy, they can recommend one ! (Watch your toes, sometimes!!)

☐   If you want to know how to raise a child – they will tell you the child's strengths and suggest supportive activities to help them grow.

Angels are support systems of the highest order, but they cannot tell you what to do or how to live, unless you ask, because you do have free will. Angels carry energy, ideas, inspiration, love, and joy from God to give to us.

DO I HAVE AN ANGEL AND HOW WILL I KNOW?

Think of a time when an idea came to you that was so vivid and pure and so true for you that rolls of shivers came over your body...you may call that angel touches or love rushes. *THAT WAS THEM !*

Think of a time when you awakened at night with a thought so clear you knew it answered every question. *THAT WAS THEM !*

Think of a time when you were so still you could hear music and knew it was the "music of the spheres and divine sounds." *THAT WAS THEM !*

Think of a time when you loved so totally that you could not express it for there were no words to translate those feelings. *THAT WAS THEM !*

Think of a time when the Earth and God and You were
so aligned that you knew it was your truth in all its
glory. ***THAT WAS THEM !***
Think of a time you were so connected with love and
light that you said you were filled with God or the
Holy Spirit –
You were there and they were too!

Angel Message

We are not hard to find
We are there in the stillness
We are there in the waiting
We are there in the knowing
We are there
Just be still and trust the moment!

A BASIC PROTECTION TECHNIQUE/PRAYER

Say aloud, "I visualize myself surrounded and encased by a beautiful, golden, iridescent white light of the Divine Source, flowing
through my head or crown chakra, filling my body in its entirety and
dispelling of all blockages and negativity.

I ask that my Angels only let through those of the Highest Vibration and Intent to come in contact with me.

I visualize this light immersing my entire body in a bubble, protecting me from harm. I am now protected and safe, only energy for my
highest and best good can enter my aura or circle of light."

So is my wish and intent and so it is!!

AMEN

Now visualize yourself inside the protective bubble of golden white
light. You are now protected by your Angels and the Divine.

Here are a few types of prayers you may use to start this process:
Remember Prayer is Just Asking. You can use God, Mother/Father
God, Angels, Universal Light, THE DIVINE, and Spirit Guides inter-
changeably, if you so desire.

Guardian Angel Prayer

Angel of God, my guardian dear,
To whom God's love commits me here,
Ever this day be at my side, To light and guard, to rule and guide.
AMEN

Another Prayer:

Dear Mother/Father God, (Angels, Guides, or Universal One)
Please help me hear you clearly through your loving angels.
Allow me to be healed in my areas of greatest need and to learn
more about your truth, love, and joy. *AMEN*

An Angel Prayer:

Angels sent by God to guide me, be my light,
and walk beside me.
Be my guardian angel and protect me,
and on the path of life direct me.
AMEN

A Daily Prayer

Dear God,
Please bring the right people, circumstances, and events into my
life today that I may better do thy will. *AMEN*

Prayer for Increased Energy

Archangel Michael,
I ask you and your helpers to come to me now.
Please cut away and release anything that is draining me.
Help to lift my energy to its natural state of vitality now.
Thank You.

Prayer To Heal Parent-Child Relationship
Dear Mother/Father God,
Please help myself and my child have a harmonious relationship. I ask for your help in healing any fears that interfere with my child and me expressing love to one another.
Please help my child to focus and feel happy.
Please help my child accept my circumstances and me. I ask that You and the Angels help my child and I release our unforgivingness and resentment.
Please help us have a loving and close relationship. *AMEN*

Prayer to Attract New Friends
Dear God and Angels Above,
I now see myself surrounded by loving friends with whom I share much in common. I can feel the presence of new friendships with like-minded souls, and I ask Your help in manifesting this vision.
Please guide me to meet new people who are positive, spiritually minded, health conscious and fun. Please help me to know that I deserve the love and attention of these new friends. Thank you so much. *AMEN*

A Healing Prayer
Dear Angels,
Please surround me with your healing energy, and help me to heal my craving for unhealthful foods and drinks.
Please remove my desire for toxic substances and help me to have the motivation to live and eat healthfully.
Please guide me while shopping, preparing, and eating food, and give me guidance about how to live without polluting myself or my world.
With great love and gratitude, I thank you. *AMEN*

Prayer for Health and Healing
Dear God,
I know that You created me in the perfect image and likeness of
Yourself.
I ask that you, Holy Spirit, and the Archangel Raphael help me
know and experience this health in my physical body.
I am willing to release all thoughts and behaviors that create the
illusion of illness and pain. I know that You are omnipresent, so
therefore, You exist in every cell in my body. Please help me feel
Your love in my physical body, so that I can know that You cradle
me in Your arms right now. *AMEN*

Prayer for Sleep Issues
To My Creator,
Please help me to have a restful and sound sleep tonight.
I ask for a guardian angel to be posted on the north, south, east
and west sides of my home during the night.
I visualize my home surrounded by the Divine White Light of
Your Protective Love.
I am willing to release all of my cares and worries to You and the
Angels, so that the pockets of my soul are emptied for the night.
Please send some comforting angels to my side, so that I may en-
joy a wonderful night's sleep. *AMEN*

Prayer for Finding Your Life Purpose
To Everyone Who Watches Over Me,
I seem to have forgotten my Divine Life Purpose,
and I ask your help so that I may remember the reason
I chose to come here at this time.
I am willing to release all fears that keep me from remembering-
my life's purpose, including the
fear of success and failure.
I know that I am qualified to fulfill my mission,
and I ask for your continued guidance in helping me
to know which path makes my heart sing.
Please help me to know the difference between joy and fear so
that I may immerse myself in meaningful actions that serves others
and brings me joy. Thank you so much. *AMEN*

A Prayer for Peace
St. Francis of Assisi

Lord, make me an instrument of thy peace.
Where there is hatred, let me sow love;
Where there is injury, pardon;
Where there is discord, union;
Where there is doubt, faith;
Where there is despair, hope;
Where there is darkness, light;
Where there is sadness, joy.

O Divine Master, grant me that I
May not so much seek
To be consoled, as to console;
To be understood, as to understand;
To be loved, as to love.
For it is in giving that we receive;
It is in pardoning that we are pardoned;
And it is in dying that we are born to eternal life.

Here's What the Angels Want You to Know:

That all is well and that you are well protected. Yes, you have much to do, and we can help you. **ASK.**

Ask for *Angels of Organization* to come to you and help you today.

Ask for *Angels of Understanding* to come to you. They have peace for you.

Ask for the *Angels of Wisdom* to come to you that you may better understand your work.

Ask for the *Angels of Clarity* to come to you that you may understand yourself and others.

Ask for the *Angels of Patience* to come to you that you may follow divine right order.

Ask for the *Angels of Kindness* to come to you that you may teach and heal lovingly and patiently.

Ask for the *Angels of Goodness* to come to you that you will see it in others and exude it from yourself.

Ask for the *Angels of Timeliness* to come to you that you may better flow with your own synchronicity.

Ask for the *Angels of Beingness* to be with you that you may find joy in your existence.

Ask for the *Angels of Knowledge* to come to you that you may understand your work.

Ask for the *Angels of Healing* to come to you that your teachings will
help others on every level of body, mind, and spirit.

Ask for the *Angels of Discernment* to come to you
so that you may see what is truly important.

And above all, Ask for the *Angels of Love* to come to you
that you may walk in the heart of God.

This is what you will do today. We love you and all is well.

Your Angels

Prayer of Daily Manifestation
Every thing in every way, Every part of every day
Manifests by what I think, do and say.
Thank heavens I'm ONE with GOD/ MOTHER/FATHER GOD/
THE DIVINE / THE UNIVERSE TODAY!

WHY PEOPLE DON'T ASK MOTHER/ FATHER GOD OR DIVINE
FOR HELP – TOTAL MISCONCEPTIONS

- "I was taught asking for anything for myself is selfish."
- "I might get what I want and then have to 'deal' with it."
- "I might pray or ask wrong, or ask for the wrong thing in the wrong way."
- "Prayer didn't work for me before! God doesn't hear me."
- "Material things are evil or bad. Rich people don't get to heaven."
- "If I get 'good things' I'll also have to take 'bad things' too."
- "I don't deserve anything."
- "God is busy. He doesn't need to be bothered with my stresses and worries."
- "I haven't prayed for a while, so why would God listen to me now?"
- "God is up there somewhere, and I am down here and unimportant compared to all the issues he needs to deal with. Look at the global problems; they are bigger than mine!"

And the truth of the matter is…God has a plan for each and every one of us. Angels do God's will and that God is truly a loving, caring God. We can make up with God through our angels, without fear of punishment of any kind.

GOOD ADVICE TO FOLLOW:

Do what you need to do to help yourself. Be nice to yourself. But most of all **ASK** your angels for help. **BELIEVE** they are helping and guiding you along the path. **LET GO** because you do not have to do it by yourself or alone. Actually *alone* spelled properly (divine vocabulary) is really spelled *ALL-ONE*! And then say **THANK YOU** for your angels' love and guidance, even if you don't feel, see, or hear them at that time.

THEY ARE THERE FOR YOU,

BUT….

YOU HAVE TO INVITE THEM INTO YOUR HEART

AND INTO YOUR LIFE.

ASK AND YOU WILL RECEIVE.

Asking is the invitation for the angels to go to work for you. If you never ask for yourself, no matter how material it is, you will never learn how good angels are and how much they love you! In the Bible, it is referenced in James 4:2: "You have not, because you ask not!"

TEACH ME ANGELS…. HOW DO I ASK?

TO BE: ask for help in achieving personal goals. What is your heart's desire? What is the most outrageous thought of what you could ever aspire? Ask, "Angels, help me be more honest," or "Angels, help me be the best runner I can be."

TO DO: What do you love to do so much that you would do it for free? What do you love so much that you would stay up all night to do it? What can't you wait to get home from work to do? Of which experiences of your life do you tell stories? Ask for help in the activity.

Say, "Angels, please help me get into medical school," or "Angels, please help me paint the prettiest picture."

TO HAVE: What do you frequently dream about having? What are your favorite pages in a catalog? What home, car, vacation, or hobby do you fantasize about most? Ask for a particular item or event, such as, "Angels, please help me find a new apartment, new outfit, perfect for me and my needs," or "Angels, please help me find a reliable car, that will encompass all my needs and desires."

KNOW THIS: What you love to do most contains your life's purpose!! Your passion is your path. By working in areas that fulfill you and excite you, by doing what you truly love, you will flow into your life's work and will not have to seek it. It will find you!!

ANGEL MESSAGE
YOU ARE NEVER ALONE
WE TEACH YOU
WE HEAL YOU
WE GUIDE AND SUPPORT YOU
WE PROTECT YOU
WE WALK WITH YOU IN LOVE

Positive Angel Affirmations:
I am now surrounded by angels.
The angels shine the love of God upon me and through me
I accept this love from God and the Angels.
I deserve love,
I deserve happiness,
I deserve health,
I deserve help from heaven, and I accept it now.
I call upon God and the angels to help and guide me.
I listen to my inner voice and feelings.
My inner voice and feelings are guidance from God and the Angels.
This guidance is everything I need;
I follow my guidance in full faith;
I know that God and the Angels love me
and are guiding me right now.

I accept the angels' love;
I accept love.
I love.
I am love.
I am loving.
I am very loved.
Everyone loves me.
I love everyone.
I forgive myself.
I send God's love to everyone I meet.
I guard my thoughts carefully and allow positive and
loving thoughts to come through.
There is an abundance of love in the world.
There is enough for everyone.
There is plenty to go around.
I have an abundance of everything.
I attract wonderful, loving people into my life.
My angels and I enjoy new opportunities to give service to the world.
I am rewarded constantly.
My life is harmonious and peaceful.
I am peaceful.
I am radiant.
I am joyful.
I love and approve of myself exactly as I am.
I have the ability to change my state of mind.
I see opportunity in everything.
I am a valuable asset to my friends and family.
I am safe and protected wherever I go.
My gifts and abilities get stronger every day.
I handle problems and adversities with ease.
I learn from every experience in my life.
I am an extremely happy person.
I accept the challenges of life and handle them with
skill and confidence.
My consistent mindful touching of people and life,
both protects me from burnout
and enhances my ability to help heal others.

I will meet people where they are, and in the meeting,
restore their life because they are met.
In order to transform others, I must first transform myself.
I have only love and compassion for others; anything else is a waste.
I can only give what I have.
Try not. Do. Or do not. There is no try.
The Force will be with me, always.
Healer, Heal Thyself.
I Can Handle It!!

Affirmations said daily will increase your self-confidence and self-love. Tape these in a prominent place that you see everyday, like your bathroom mirror or on your cosmetic table. Add you own personal affirmation related to your goals and desires to this list.

Best of luck and Remember TO ASK YOUR ANGELS FOR HELP!

Chapter Three

MEDITATION – WHAT IS IT AND HOW DO I BEGIN

There are many types of meditation. The one definition that fits almost all types is. *"Consciously directing your attention to alter your state of consciousness."* There's no limit to the things you can direct your attention toward — symbols, sounds, colors, breath, uplifting thoughts, spiritual realms, etc. Meditation is simply about attention, where you direct it, and how it alters your consciousness.

WHAT IS THE PURPOSE OF MEDITATION?

Traditionally meditation was (and still is) used for spiritual growth, becoming more in touch with our core self, our inner child, our angels, our spirit guides or higher powers. More recently, meditation has become a valuable tool for finding a peaceful oasis of relaxation and stress relief in a demanding, fast-paced world. Meditation can include visualizations, guided imagery, praying, and hypnotherapy techniques.

SOME MISCONCEPTIONS ABOUT MEDITATION

Misconception One — Meditation is turning off your thoughts or making your mind a blank.

Not True — Inner quietness is experienced in meditation, but not by willfully turning off thoughts. Quieting the mind results naturally from the effectiveness of the method used... and an uplifting spiritual energy called chi that is beyond our own efforts.

Misconception Two — Meditation is difficult and requires great concentration.

Not True — Meditation can be easily learned and practiced. Meditation is only difficult if we become too concerned with doing it correctly or incorrectly. Although staying focused in meditation does become easier with time and practice, it is definitely not a requirement for beginning to meditate. Thinking that we should be good at focusing when first starting out is essentially putting the cart before the horse.

Misconception Three — Meditation is not successful unless we see interesting things in our mind.

Not True — Although some meditations are specifically for visualizing, many are not, and it is not essential. Some people sense or feel things inwardly, and that's all right.

FREQUENTLY ASKED QUESTIONS

How often should I meditate? Optimum results come from daily practice, once or twice daily. However, you may choose to meditate on an as-needed basis.

How long should my meditations be? If you are just beginning meditation and wish to practice regularly, it is best to start meditating 10 to 15 minutes once a day. After a while, you may want to increase that to 20 to 45 minutes once a day, or 10 minutes twice a day.

What should I be experiencing when I meditate? The possible experiences when meditating are unlimited. They can range from extraordinary to ordinary; from blissful to boring; from peaceful to action packed. All of these experiences are all right and perfectly normal. The point is to accept whatever occurs in meditation. Put your expectations aside, and don't worry about doing it right. There are infinite possibilities and no fixed criterion for determining right meditation. Just remember to try not to force something to happen, or over-analyze your meditation; just be with the moment and what is meant to happen will.

The beginning steps to start to meditate can be simple to follow.

- ∞ Start by finding a quiet, comfortable place to meditate. You can sit in a comfortable chair, on the bed, on the floor...anywhere that is comfortable. It is not necessary to sit cross-legged. Your legs can be in any position that is comfortable.
- ∞ Eliminate as much noise and as many potential distractions as possible. Don't worry about those things that you cannot control.
- ∞ When you sit to meditate, sit comfortably, with your spine reasonably straight. This allows the spiritual energy to flow freely up the spine, which is an important aspect of meditation. Leaning against a chair back, a wall, or headboard is perfectly all right. If, for physical reasons, you cannot sit up, lay flat on your back.
- ∞ Place your hands in any position that is comfortable.
- ∞ Call on a "higher source" for assistance in your meditation, be that Mother/Father God, Angels, Masters, Spirit Guides, the Divine or God. Any source of higher guidance is right; it depends on with whatever you are most comfortable.

ASKING FOR SPIRITUAL HELP

1. You may like to speak these words aloud: *"I ask my Guides and Angels to help me solve the problem of... I ask that I meet up with these Higher Beings, in my dreams tonight and discuss the matter fully. I will listen to their Divine answers and advice. In the morning I will remember the dream and conversation and then decide with my own best judgment, how to act upon the problem."*

2. *Or my favorite is: "Mother/Father God, Angels, Masters, Spirit Guides above of the white light, I ask for your guidance, wisdom and unconditional love to help guide me, show me and teach me the way for my life. I ask for your presence here tonight as I meditate and pray. Please help me find answers to my questions, concerns and issues at hand — tell them your questions, concerns, and issues at hand — and then just listen...."*

3. Protect yourself spiritually, in a golden/white light, shaped like an auric egg around yourself and go to sleep.

4. In the morning when you awake, or when you return to the
   room after meditating, immediately write down any conversations you have had or thoughts that come to you into your
   dream journal.
5. If the advice seems right for you, act upon it!

*Note. Your Angels, Guides, and Masters are there in the Higher
Dimensions, to guide you on your journey through life. They are not
there to command you to do anything, as they value your freewill!

The Guardians of the Animal, Vegetation, Gem, and Nature
worlds are often called Devas or Clan Spirits or Creature Teachers. Some people in the past have called them fairies, nymphs, lep-
rechauns, trolls, elves, spirits and more. They may come into your
dreams as beautiful ethereal creatures, such as unicorns or fairies, and
they can help you link to these different spiritual realms, which exist
beyond our third dimension. They can guide you, teach you, and help
you create a rapport with animals, vegetation, gems, and the environment of your local area.

A BASIC PROTECTION TECHNIQUE

Say aloud, *"I visualize this building surrounded by a beautiful, golden,
white light, of the Divine Source, entering in through the doors and windows, filling this building in its entirety, dispelling all negativity and totally
protecting me and all within. I ask that my Spiritual Guardian only let
through those of the Highest Vibration and Intent. I state that I will always use my spiritual/psychic gifts for the Highest Good!"*

Now visualize yourself inside a protective bubble of golden, iridescent, white light. Inside this protection, at your front and rear, place a
power symbol such as a cross, a six-pointed star, or ankh, with whatever you are most comfortable. This protective bubble will deflect all
negative energies, but allows positive energies through. If you feel
unsure about any spiritual or alien beings, tell them to depart or be
gone. Repeat several times if required.

*"Do not search for us, we will find you. Do not wait for us, we are
here...all ready. Do not whisper your name, we know it well. We have
loved you forever, time will tell. We are your Guardian Angels."*

Here is a simplified version of my rainbow meditation. To hear it on audio CD, feel the vibration of the music and the angels, please order a copy of my *Angels In The Rainbow* CD. See order form in the back of the book.

Rainbow Meditation

Please make yourself comfortable, sitting or lying down
When I say inhale, take a slow deep breath,
and as you inhale, you will feel healing energy filling your body.

Allow a universal white light to start to penetrate through your head
and allow it to flow freely through every part of your body.
As you exhale, you wash away all worries, stresses, and concerns.
With each breath, you will feel more and more relaxed,
more and more centered

READY?

Now inhale, hold it, exhale...feeling it embrace you completely.
Again, inhale, hold it, exhale...blowing out all your
worries and concerns.
Once more, inhale, hold it, and exhale completely.

You are now feeling more and more relaxed,
More and more centered.
Continue to breathe slowly and deeply.
You are feeling relaxed.

Now find yourself in a beautiful field of wild flowers.
The fresh spring aroma of the flowers captures you,
The earth has absorbed a loving spring rainfall.
You are in awe by the vivid colors of the flowers,
Wearing droplets of diamonds on their petals.
With each breath, you become more a part of the universe,
More and more as one with Mother Earth.
We are One and as One we are powerful.
We allow positive thoughts to enter our minds, and

We release all stresses, worries, and concerns.
We allow our Angels to speak honestly and openly with us,
As they are our guides, our teachers and our new best friends.
We allow them to heal every aspect of our soul.

An arch of color appears...a rainbow is forming across the sky.
You watch it reach high to the heavens and
Then touch down atop a small hill ahead of you.
The colors are vivid and they shimmer and glow;
They are welcoming you.
You want to embrace them, bathe in them,
To inhale them and to make them a part of you.

Now step into the rainbow and be embraced.
You are relaxed and at peace.
You are strong, powerful, and important.
Your angels are right here with you.
You are safe, healthy, and totally free.

Each color empowers your energy centers;
Violet forms a crown for your head,
Indigo a deep violet at your forehead,
Blue spreads around your throat area,
Green centers on your chest and heart area, and you feel the love in
this room and those around you.
Yellow centers on your solar plexus and upper abdominal area,
Orange centers on the area, just below your belly button,
Red spreads into the bottom area of your spine,
Grounding and centering you to Mother Earth.
Now you are one with your rainbow and your Angels.
Feel the energy as it embraces you, welcomes you
And loves you unconditionally.
The Angels give you a warm, loving hug.
You are filled with Divine loving energy,
You are now loved and protected.

You may stay and enjoy the moment,
Speak and listen to your Angels for as long as you like,

Wait 15-20 minutes....

When you are ready...Step out of the rainbow, feeling healed,
loved and at peace.

You can come back here anytime you want to
and communicate with your Angels and Guides.

On the count of 5 you will awaken, feeling loved, healed,
and touched by an Angel.

1) Return to the room.
2) Take some deep breaths.
3) Start to stir and feel your fingers and toes.
4) Prepare to open your eyes.
5) Open your eyes and begin to write what you saw, felt, or heard.
ENJOY!!

SANCTUARY MEDITATION (INTRODUCTION)

Here is a simplified version of *Finding Sanctuary,* written and spoken by Brian Dean. .

Sanctuary Meditation

The meditation you are about to undertake is called *Finding Sanctuary,* and is a calming, peaceful experience. A sanctuary is a place of calm, a place to go to when things in your life become too stressful. Visiting your sanctuary is like taking a small vacation within yourself, going to a nice calm restful place, and recharging your batteries. You release all the tensions that have built up over time, and refresh yourself in the calm peacefulness of your inner surroundings. It can also be a place of wonder and enjoyment. It can be a place of excitement where you can release all the tensions and have fun.

Your sanctuary can be many things. It is a place of your creation.

Within it are the things you need to feel calm and refreshed, to lose any tension you have built up. Your sanctuary is a pleasant environment, and visiting it is always a happy, restful experience. In a few moments, you will be creating your sanctuary, but don't go there with any pre-conceived notions. Your sanctuary is actually created in your sub-conscious mind, not your conscious. Don't picture something, and say, "I want this to be in my sanctuary." What you find in your sanctuary will be exactly what you need to calm and re-energize. As your subconscious is creating this place of calm, it knows what you need most.

Close your eyes.

Take another breath, let it out.

Let your mind float for a moment, let it float and center itself.

Bring in the colors that correspond with the seven chakras. One by one, bring in the red, orange, yellow, green, blue, indigo and violet. Let them swirl inside of you, and then let them out into your aura.

I am going to count from ten to one. With each level you will feel yourself sink, going deeper.

Ten, going deep.
Deeper still, nine.
Ten times deeper, eight.
Seven.
Twenty times deeper, six.
Five.
Thirty times deeper, four.
Feeling safe and protected three.
Ten times deeper, two.
And one.

Take the colors in your aura, and weave them into a small carpet capable of carrying you to where you want to go. Step onto your carpet, sit down, and fasten your seat belt.

Now, slowly, your carpet starts to rise. Higher it goes, until you are flying through the clouds. Up ahead, you will see a violet-colored cloud. You enter the cloud, feeling the vibration of violet as you fly through it. When you emerge on the other side of the cloud, you look below; you see a stream with a small sandy clearing. Your carpet starts descending, heading toward the clearing. There, it gently lands. Step off your carpet. It will remain here until you return.

In front of you is a small stream. The water is peacefully flowing by at slow pace. Walk down though the clearing to the edge of the stream. Slowly, step into the warm, burbling water, and wade out to the center. The water is not deep, and only comes a few inches above your ankles.

Turn downstream and walk for a while. As you walk, you will notice that the sun is shining, and feels warm on your body. You can feel the slight breeze as warm air passes by you. Along each bank, there are trees and other vegetation. You can see leaves gently moving as the breeze touches them. You can hear the leaves rustling, and the song of birds up in the trees.

After a moment, you see a bend in the stream. At the top of the bend is a small sandy clearing. At the top of the clearing is a path through the trees. Leave the stream, and walk into the clearing, and head for the path. As you walk the path, you will see that there is a small hill ahead. It is a gentle slope, and the height is only about ten feet. Stop at the bottom of the hill. On the other side of that hill, is your sanctuary.

In a moment, you will walk up the hill, and enter your sanctuary. What you will find there, is of your own creation. Whatever makes you calm and feel at ease, will be there.

Maybe you like wooded areas or grassy fields. Or maybe you like quiet ponds or the beach. Maybe you're most comfortable around rocky deserts or mountains. Whatever you find most calming, you will find in your sanctuary. Remember, your sanctuary is a vast place, and you may find different types of areas in the different parts of it. You will also find other things that make you most comfortable and relaxed. If you feel relaxed at the side of a pond, you may find a comfortable couch there waiting for you. You may take a stroll in a grassy field and find a quaint, comfortable house.

You may ask the universe if it has any message for you. These messages could appear in any form. You may find a mailbox nearby, or a computer with e-mail, or a bottle with a message in it. Again, whatever you feel most comfortable with is what you will find. Don't create a picture before you walk in, just let it appear, and see it as it is.

Remember, everything you will find will be peaceful. You are always safe and protected in your sanctuary. No one else may enter unless you invite them.

OK. Now walk up the hill and into your sanctuary. Discover its wonders. Feel free to explore, or just relax.

Wait 15 minutes, then continue...

It is now time to return. Come back to the entrance of your sanctuary. You may return here anytime you like. It will always be here, and it will always be relaxing and restful. Now, walk down the hill, into the clearing and back into the stream, heading back the way you came. The water is still warm, and the breeze is still blowing gently. As you approach the rock you laid on before, you walk around it. A little bit further, you see the clearing that you started from, and your carpet is still there waiting for you. Leave the stream, and walk up into the clearing.

Sit down on your carpet, and settle back into it. As you do, it starts to rise, and heads away from the stream. It rises up and flies through the clouds. You see the violet cloud ahead and enter it. As you come out the other side, you are back in the world you left. Slowly, you start to descend. You pick up speed and begin to sink quickly, yet smoothly. You come down, closer and closer to the place you started from. Your carpet slows, and gently settles on the floor here. Get up off your carpet, roll it up, and set it aside. It will be there when you want it again.

I am going to count from one to ten. With each level, you will feel yourself coming closer, until you are at the place you started from.

One, coming closer.
Getting nearer, two.
Three.
Coming back with lots of energy, four.
Coming back feeling good, feeling relaxed, five.
Getting closer still, six.
Approaching now, safe and protected, seven.
Coming back feeling good, full of energy, loved, eight.
Almost back, nine.
And you are now back, ten.

Take a deep breath, and open your eyes when you are ready. You have successfully completed a journey into your sanctuary. You have returned rested, relaxed, and full of energy. You may make this journey any time you want. Just go through this same meditation to get you there and bring you back.

A Prayer For All

Mother-Father-God,
I ask you to bless my friends that read or hear these
    words now.
I am asking you to minister to their spirit at this very mo-
    ment.
Where there is pain, give them Your peace and mercy.
Where there is self-doubting,
release a renewed confidence in Your ability to work
    through them.
Where there is tiredness, or exhaustion,
I ask You to give them understanding, patience, and
    strength as they learn submission to your leading.
Where there is spiritual stagnation, I ask You to renew
    them by revealing Your nearness, and by drawing
    them into greater intimacy with You.
Where there is fear, reveal Your loveand release to them
    Your courage.
Where there is a sin blocking them,reveal it and break its
    hold over their life.
Bless their finances. Give them greater vision and raise
    up leaders and friends to support and encourage
    them.
Give each of them discernment to recognize the evil
    forces around them, and reveal to them the power
    they have in You to defeat it.
I ask You to do these things in Your name.
    AMEN

Teach Me to Pray ...
Virginia Ellis

Please teach me, Lord ...
I want to know exactly how to pray.
I need some words, which ones are right?
Please tell me what to say.

I've bowed my head, I have knelt down,
But ... should I be upright?
I've closed my eyes, I've raised my hands,
Or ... should I fold them tight?

Do I stand up? Should I sit down?
Dear Lord ... what do you like?
Are lights turned on or are they off?
Maybe ... candle light?

Wear my glasses? Take them off?
Be at my desk or table? Should I
whisper? Speak out loud?
Do I quote the Bible?

What do you think about the time? Do you
prefer the dawn?
Should I pray fast, or keep it slow?
Better short...or long?

I'm new at this, what are the rules?
I want to do it right.
How do I know You'll even hear that I am in Your sight?

And while I sat there quietly, Waiting for some sign,
I heard a gentle voice say,

"Oh, dearest child of mine ...
Do you think I really care about the time of day,

Or whether you are standing up, or kneeling when you pray?"
"I don't care about your posture, or about the place you choose;
Just open up your soul to me, I have no other rules.
Tell me what is in your heart, and tell me what you seek;
Tell me of your sorrows, and of those things that made you weak."

"Speak to me in private about what concerns you most;
I know about your good deeds...you have no need to boast.
My child, you don't need lessons, just talk to me each day;
Tell me anything you want, dear child,
Anyone can pray."
AMEN

Here are some great children's prayers I found. You don't have
to be a kid to say or use them, but I thought they were good starting
prayers, hope they help !

A Child's Prayer For Morning
My God,
I offer to You this day all I think or do or say, in union with all
You have done for me by Jesus Christ Your Son.
Amen.

Dear Lord, I rise from bed to pray;
then soon go out to school or play.
Let all I meet along the way,
see You in me throughout the day.
Amen.

Angel of God
Angel of God, my Guardian Dear
To whom His love commits me here
Ever this day, be at my side,
To light and guard, To rule and guide.
Amen

I Give Today

Oh, Jesus, I give you today, all that I think and do and say,
Oh, Jesus, I love you and pray more love today than yesterday,
Oh, God, be with me I pray, be by my side forever to stay.
Amen

Prayer Before Meals

Bless us, O Lord, and these Your gifts,
which we are about to receive from Your bounty.
Through Christ our Lord.
Amen.

Now I Lay Me Down to Sleep

Now I lay me down to sleep;
I pray the Lord my soul to keep.
If I should die before I wake,
I pray the Lord my soul to take.

Night Time Prayers

Time has come for me to sleep,
And I thank Thee for Thy keep.
Watch this night well over me
Teach me Lord to trust in Thee.

Many sins I've done today
Please, Lord take them all away.
Look upon me in Thy grace
Make me pure before Thy face.

Care for children sick and poor,
Grant them Lord Thy blessing more
Care for Mom and Dad the same
This I pray in Jesus' Name.
Amen

MORNING PRAYERS

Take Care of Me

Each morning when I wake, I say
Take Care of me, Dear God, Today
In work and play, please let me be,
Always Jesus, just for Thee.
In all I think, and do and say
Take Care of me, Dear God, I pray.
Amen

Angel of God

Angel of God, my Guardian Dear
To whom His love commits me here
Ever this day, be at my side,
To light and guard
To rule and guide.
Amen

EVENING PRAYERS

Now I Lay Me Down To Sleep

Now I lay me down to sleep,
Let 14 angels watch over me,
2 at my right, 2 at my left
2 at my head, 2 at my feet
2 that will cover me
2 that will wake me and
2 that will take me to heaven
where angels sing joyfully forever,
Amen

Dear Guardian Angel

Dear Guardian Angel, thank you for keeping me safe
and helping me be a good boy today,
Help me pay attention to Mommy and Daddy or whoever's looking
after me all day tomorrow
Amen

The ABC's Of Life

Although things are not perfect
Because of trial or pain
Continue in thanksgiving
Do not begin to blame
Even when the times are hard
Fierce winds are bound to blow
God is forever able
Hold on to what you know
Imagine life without His love
Joy would cease to be
Keep thanking Him for all the things
Love imparts to thee
Move out of "Camp Complaining"
No weapon that is known
On earth can yield the power
Praise can do alone
Quit looking at the future
Redeem the time at hand
Start every day with worship
To "thank" is a command
Until we see Him coming
Victorious in the sky
We'll run the race with gratitude
Xalting God most high
Yes, there'll be good times and yes some will be bad,
but...
Zion waits in glory...where none are ever sad!

DISCOVERING YOUR LIFE PATH

To discover what your gifts or talents are, read the following question and write down your answer.

Which TEN activities do I perform, in a normal week (when I'm not depressed), that give me the most amount of personal enjoyment and fun?

As a tip they could include:
  A. Talking, socializing, or entertaining people
  B. Dancing or acting
  C. Painting or drawing
  D. Surfing the Internet
  E. Creative writing
  F. Learning how to develop my spiritual and psychic abilities
  G. Watching television
  H. Gardening or caring for the environment
  I.   Caring for animals
  J.   Caring for aged, infirm, or handicapped people
  K. Playing a musical instrument
  L. Reading about subjects that interest me, like Psychology and Sociology
  M. Exercising at the gym or going for a bicycle ride
  N. Going to the movies or watching a movie at home
  O. Listening to music
  P. Going out dancing
  Q. Cooking a gourmet meal

Now from Your list, rate them in order of preference, with number one being the highest and number ten being the lowest. Rate them on, how much enjoyment and inner fulfillment they give you when you are performing that activity. Once you have done this, remove numbers nine and ten from the list.

Begin to reassess and change the order of your preferences, if necessary. Each day, remove two more numbers from the list. Continue, to reassess your list, until you only have numbers one and two left. If you have been honest with yourself and have carefully followed the above instructions, the last two remaining items on the list are the activities in life that give you the most amount of enjoyment and inner fulfillment.

Once you know this, you can be certain that the activities that you are left with, numbers one and two are your personal gifts to humanity or world plan aims. The next step is to carefully look at your two chosen activities, numbers one and two, and write out a list of all the professions or jobs you can think of that include these activities.

An example of this could be, that you like painting and caring for animals. Therefore, how about becoming a pet portrait artist? Or you like developing your psychic and spiritual abilities and caring for people. With a little thought, it is easy to work out the ideal profession or job for yourself.

It is recommended that you start your new career as either a hobby or a voluntary part time commitment. This will give you the opportunity to try it, before totally committing yourself to the new career choice.

If you discover that your new hobby or part time commitment is not the ideal career choice for yourself, redo the above exercise. This time, include in the second exercise, some of the new skills and activities that you currently like to perform in your hobby. This will make your second attempt at the exercise, more accurate. Then decide which other hobby or part time work commitment would you like to attempt.

Continue to redo the exercise, as many times as necessary. Persist in changing your hobby or part time commitment, until you discover the ideal career opportunity for yourself. The tiny amount of effort that you have to put into discovering it is nothing, compared to the amount of personal pleasure and inner fulfillment it will give you for the rest of your life!

Now, you should have realized, that by discovering what your Life Path Plan is and making it a major component of your life or chosen career, you will be getting paid to perform the activity that gives you the most amount of pleasure and inner fulfillment! No longer will your work or career be mind numbing. It will be like love — you will never be able to get enough of it!

Slow Down Therapy

Slow down; God is still in heaven. You are not responsible for doing it all yourself, right now.

Remember a happy, peaceful time in your past. Rest
there. Each moment has richness that takes a lifetime
to savor.

Set your own pace. When someone is pushing you, it's
OK to tell them they're pushing

Take nothing for granted: watch water flow, the corn
grow, the leaves blow, your neighbor mow. Taste your
food. God gives us food for pure delight as well as to
nourish.

Notice the sun and the moon as they rise and set. They
are remarkable for their steady pattern of movement,
not their speed.

Quit planning how you're going to use what you know,
learn, or possess. God's gifts just are. Be grateful and
their purpose will be clear.

Talk and play with children. It will bring out the playful
and unhurried little person inside you.

When you talk with someone, don't think about what
you'll say next. Thoughts will spring up naturally if
you let them.

Create a place in your home...at your work...in your
heart...where you can go for quiet and recollection.
You deserve it.

Allow yourself time to be lazy and unproductive. Rest isn't a luxury, it's a necessity.

Listen to the wind blow. It carries a message of yesterday and tomorrow and now. NOW counts. NOW is a present from God.

Rest on your laurels. They bring comfort whatever their size, age, or condition. Talk slower. Talk less. Don't talk. Communication isn't measured by words.

Give yourself permission to be late sometimes. Life is for living, not scheduling.

Listen to the song of a bird; the complete song. Music and nature are gifts, but only if you are willing to receive them.

Take time just to think. Action is good and necessary, but it's fruitful only if we muse, ponder, and mull.

Make time for play — and to do the things you like to do. Whatever your age, your inner child needs recreation.

Watch and listen to the night sky. It speaks. Listen to the words you speak, especially in prayer.

Learn to stand back and let others take their turn as leaders. There will always be new opportunities for you to step out in front again.

Divide big jobs into little jobs. If God took six days to create the universe, can you hope to do any better?

When you find yourself rushing and anxious, STOP. Ask
yourself "WHY" you are rushing and anxious. The
reasons may improve your self-understanding.

Take time to read the Bible or another Holy Book.
Thoughtful reading is enriching reading.

Count your blessings — slowly, one at a time.
Count your friends. If you have one, you are lucky. If
you have more, you are blessed. Bless them in return.

Take a day off alone; make a retreat. You can learn
from monks and hermits without becoming one.

Pet a furry friend. You will give and get the gift of love.
Work with your hands. It frees the mind. Take time
to wonder. Without wonder, life is merely existence.

Sit in the dark. It will teach you to see and hear, taste
and smell. Once in a while, turn down the lights, the
volume, the throttle, the invitations. Less really can
be more.

Let go. Nothing is usually the hardest thing to do but
often it is the best. Take a walk — but don't go anywhere. If you walk just to get somewhere, you sacri-
fice the walking.

Direct your life with purposeful choices, not with speed
and efficiency. The best musician is one, who plays
with expression and meaning, not the one who
finishes first.

Chapter Four

Color Energy and How Colors can Empower our Life

olor and light are inseparable. Each color of the visible light rays has a different wavelength and vibrational frequency, which affects us differently. Red has the longest wavelength and the slowest vibrational frequency, which we recognize as warm and stimulating; however, violet has the shortest wavelength and the fastest frequency, which we recognize as a cool and calming energy. We receive light and color information through our eyes, which then stimulates the retina and its cells, rods and cones. These "color" impulses travel through the optic nerve to the visual cortex of the brain via the pituitary, triggering other glands and their hormone secretion to other parts of the body. Light rays consist of the seven color energies: red, orange, yellow, green, blue, indigo, and violet. We can see these seven colors in a rainbow, drop of rain or dew, and even in a snowflake.

Many body functions are stimulated or retarded by light and the different colors of light. Since light and its colors physically affect glands and hormones, they will also have a marked influence on our moods and feelings. Science has proven that certain colors can calm the mind while others stimulate mental activity. We need light energy for nourishing our brain, our emotions, and our physical body. Light can also enter through our skin and our breath. As well, we can receive additional color energy through a balance of various colored foods, herbs, vitamins, aromatherapy, sound, minerals, clothing, decor, and color bathing.

HOW DOES COLOR AFFECT YOU?

Most people don't realize the power of color, yet. Think of when you eat certain foods or take a vitamin. Do you really know how it affects your whole system — body, mind, and spirit? Probably not. To understand the effect of something you have to educate yourself and study its effects. For example, to learn how color affects, you try bringing in a color's power by using different tools. Note things like, what is the best way for you to feel a color's energy (bathing in a color, eating foods of a specific color, wearing a color, etc.); through what senses are you best stimulated; and how long do you need to use a color to notice its affects. Color has been proven to have various results on your mood and physical level. Color is a fun and effective way to influence you. And remember it is even quoted in the scriptures: "Let there be light." Light is color and color is light, so give it a try!

We all use color therapy in our daily life through the foods we eat to the clothes we wear. However, our environment inundates us with several colors at a time and therefore does not always recognize the full potential of using only one color. By focusing on the power of only one energy for a day, week or even a month will help you understand more about your own chakra centers and how you can empower yourself with whatever energy you need at any given time.

If you really want to understand what color can do and how it can charge your energy and chakras, try the following exercise. Begin your day taking an organic and energizing RED Color Bath™ or a RED foot bath. You can intensify the power of your RED bath experience by adding a few drops of either ylang ylang or sandalwood oil. Next envision the vitality of the RED ray entering your feet and stimulating your life vitality — your chi flow. Direct the RED energy into your root center and feel yourself grounded and connected to the Earth and your existence. Feel the power of the RED energy giving you its confidence and inner strength. After your morning "color treatment" drink a glass of RED cranberry or RED tomato juice or have a cup of RED zinger, ginseng, or cranberry tea. For the day, wear a piece of

RED clothing whether it is a RED top, RED scarf, RED underwear, or RED socks. I have been told Color Energy has probably increased the sales of RED underwear in North America! You can even put a RED gemstone in your pocket or play some RED music.

For example, when I do my red, power shower I envision the power of the RED coming up my legs through the reflex zones in my feet. I see the RED energy giving me its vitality and strength to accomplish my goals of the day. I feel its passion and its courage connect to my being allowing me to walk forward in life with confidence and self-esteem. Spiritually I know I exist and am part of the universal flow in my physical body. I feel the power of the RED strengthening my back and reproductive system and also giving me the foundation and support to accomplish my heart's desires. And for fun at the end of my shower, I release any negative attachments of anger or unwanted aggression, which I no longer want and still may be unconsciously hidden.

When you bring in a power, you have a choice on how you want to use it! So use it to have a good and fun day and use it to empower yourself! And remember if it has taken you a lifetime to acquire your energy to the point that it is today. It may take you a while to shift your energy to the optimal level that it can be. It's like school. If you are not so good in one subject you may not pass to the next grade level. Similarly if one chakra center is not so strong, you have to do homework to build up your knowledge and understanding of it.

One of the things I try to teach people is that you have a choice everyday on what type of day you would like to have. This means you can choose to have a great day or a not so great day. Some mornings it is a little bit more difficult to think that this is possible, but it is. Every morning imagine kick starting your day with some vitality and some fantastic positive thoughts. As you are the master of your own domain, it is up to you to do something to make your day be the best it can possibly be. But it you don't put 100 percent of yourself into this morning ritual, I guarantee you that your day may not be filled with wonder. Also remember that "color tools" work on an unconscious level, helping you to achieve your goals.

What I suggest is that either the night before or first thing when you wake up, plan what energy you need. I recommend the more stimulating colors of red, orange, or yellow in the morning to get you going and help you last throughout the day. Start the shower, plug the drain, and pour a little bit of the Color Bath into your water. Next envision the power of that color invigorating its connecting chakra center–feeding it the vitality you need to have your great day. If you specifically think of the traits from the color that you would like then there is even more power in its energy. Following your power shower eat the same colored foods or drink its energy through a juice. Even dress in that color or listen to the chakra song in our chakra CD, _Through the Rainbow_ or Acaysha's _Angels In The Rainbow_ CD.

Alternative medicine is one of the fastest growing areas around the world. Energy and vibrational healing is becoming more commonly used by many people and in many health professions. Colour Energy Corporation is a leader in educating and offering easy to use tools to help people access their full potential. Colour Energy products were created to help you and your clients/customers manifest changes on a conscious and unconscious level, thereby energetically empowering yourself.

Energy tools are important since we do not always live in the present time that governs our conscious self. In order to manifest a shift in one's energy field it is said one must concentrate on what it is that he or she wants to change for 57 seconds and he or she must focus on this thought several times in order to manifest it into reality. However, most people only hold a thought for three seconds!!! For example, if you bathe in a color vibration for 30 minutes that is 1,800 seconds you are programming your body with what is that you want to improve. Imagine adding the power of your correlating thoughts while doing this! It is so easy to do and very simple to incorporate as a daily or weekly ritual.

Many people have difficulty keeping focused and others have difficulties meditating or taking the time for themselves and so by using color therapy tools on a regular basis, it will encourage anyone to consciously and unconsciously raise their "vibrations" into more a positive state, which in turn will align and balance their energy centers and attract good things. The Law of Attraction says that what you give out is what you will get back! Consciously create the life you want!

Exploring Chakras and Colors

CHAKRAS

The chakras (pronounced shock-rahs) are the seven major energy points in the body. Each point controls different parts of the body as well as different functions. For example, the root chakra located at the pubic bone controls all bodily functions in that area, as well as the legs, knees, and feet. If one has physical problems with the knees or the feet, the root chakra is probably out of balance or blocked.

Each chakra also controls various functions such as thinking, communication, and balance. For each chakra, there is a color associated with it. The chart below shows each chakra along with its associated functions and colors.

Chakra (from bottom to top)	Location	Controlling Function	Color
Root	At the pubic bone where the genitals are. (The male root chakra is actually two inches lower than the female.)	Physical attributes and abilities	Red
Spleen	The midsection two inches below the naval (also known as the center).	Emotions	Orange
Solar Plexus	The sternum just below the rib cage.	Thinking (all thought processes)	Yellow
Heart	In the center of the chest.	Balance, as it is a balance point between the upper and lower chakras	Green
Throat	In the center of the throat.	Communication	Blue
Third Eye	The center of the forehead.	Insight (intuition)	Indigo (Blue / Violet)
Crown	The top of the head.	Global consciousness (connection to the Universe).	Violet

The colors of the chakras are, for the most part, based on primary colors. An easy way to remember them is to start at the root chakra, working to the crown, and take the first letter of each color to create the name Roy G. Biv (Red, Orange, Yellow, Green, Blue, Indigo, Violet). This should be familiar to anyone that took any art class that dealt with color.

RED – The Root Chakra is connected to our physical body and action. Some of its qualities are motivation, passion, and strength. Red helps to give us vitality, courage, inner strength, self-confidence and encourages us to achieve our goals. It gives us the power and inner strength to pursue our dreams. Use red if you are tired, cold, and anemic or have a lower backache. Also eases rheumatism and arthritis and stimulates circulation.

ORANGE – The Spleen Chakra is connected to our emotional and feeling self. Some of its qualities are joy, happiness, and being sociable. Orange helps with depression and releasing anxieties. Orange increases the intake of oxygen and heals and stimulates the lungs, which is ideal after an operation to give an increase in oxygen intake and helps heal more quickly. Use orange for allergies, yeast infections, hiccups, removing gas from the digestive tract, menstrual cramps, and problems with the spleen.

YELLOW – The Solar Plexus Chakra is connected to our mental and thinking self. Some of its qualities are optimism, intelligence, and being mentally creative. Yellow helps with memory, mental fatigue, nervousness, and clarity. Use yellow for digestive and liver problems, diabetes, weight problems (loss or gain), and parasites.

GREEN – The Heart Chakra is connected to our loving self. Some of its qualities are harmony, kindness, sensitivity, emotional balancing, unconditional love, understanding, and growth. Use green to calm down and bring peace into yourself. Green works on the heart, lungs, thymus gland, immune system, and blood circulation. Helps to relax muscles, nerves, thoughts, and aids in prosperity

BLUE – The Throat Chakra is connected to our expressive self. Some of its qualities are honesty, politeness, creative self-expression, and free will along with detailed planning and organizing. Use blue to soothe tired nerves, insomnia, and hyperactivity. It helps with communication, holistic thoughts, stability, fevers, and menstrual issues. Blue aids in mental relaxation, giving peace of mind.

INDIGO – The Brow Chakra is connected to our Universal seeing self. Some of the qualities are wisdom, truth seeking, and intuition.

Indigo is related to the pineal gland, inner vision, and the imagination. It is used to heal the etheric body and our aura. It helps with hearing and sleeping disorders, can be used to increase dream activity, and helps to remember dreams. Indigo purifies the blood system, calms the nerves, and cleanses the lymphatic system. It also relieves pain and skin problems.

VIOLET – The Crown Chakra is connected to our higher conscious knowing and spiritual self. Some of the qualities are inspiration, charisma, and the ability to see beauty in life. It helps to purify thoughts and feelings and increases artistic and creative abilities. Da Vinci and Einstein used the violet energy for inspiration in their research and inventions. It is used to stimulate the endocrine, lymphatic, and central nervous systems. It also helps kill bacteria and heal skin rashes.

AN EXERCISE TO STIMULATE ALL YOUR COLORS AND CHAKRA CENTERS

1. To bring your awareness to the physical level or the RED energy. Feel yourself being solid in the world. You can ask yourself why am I here or what is my purpose. Feel that you exist in your RED body.
2. Breathe in life's joy or the ORANGE energy. Slow yourself down by breathing smoothly and deeply. Choose what you want to feel with each breathe inhale. Exhale any uncomfortable feelings. Remember to keep breathing and move the energy in and out. Consciously release any negative feelings that are hidden or stuck in your body.
3. Become aware of your thoughts. The intellect is the YELLOW energy. Are you choosing your thoughts? Are they empowering? Gently guide and lead your thoughts to where you would like them to be. Know that what you believe as truth will become your truth, so choose what you decide to believe.
4. Create harmony and balance in your life or the GREEN energy. Be around nature or nurture yourself in a Green Color Bath. Develop the qualities in yourself that you want to receive from others so you will magnetize them from your relationships. Make the decision to allow yourself to receive.

5. Express yourself through the BLUE energy. Look at every situation in life as an opportunity for yourself and everyone you come in contact with. Even saying "no" to someone is an opportunity. It is an opportunity for you to set boundaries and trust yourself, and for the other person to deal with their decisions and for them to make their own empowering choices

6. Use your intuitive abilities and your empathy or the INDIGO energy, in an honoring respectful way, especially to yourself. Again choose the most empowering path you can foresee, and focus your energy on that.

7. Expand your vision of yourself and feel that wonderful energy of inspiration or the VIOLET energy and take yourself to even higher levels of living the life you are consciously creating.

THE DIFFERENT COLORS AND THEIR ENERGIES

RED   VITALITY, COURAGE, SELF CONFIDENCE

Use when you need to meet a demanding day, or when you feel drained of energy. The color red provides the power from the earth and gives energy on all levels. It connects us to our physical body. Everything that is to be commenced needs the life vitality of red.

Personality Traits: Courageous, confident, humanistic, strong-willed, spontaneous, honest, and extroverted.

The Root Chakra is governed by the red energy.

Crystals / Stones: Bloodstone, jasper, ruby, garnet, hematite, and lodestone.

Scents: Patchouli and ginger

The Archangel: Sandaphon

ORANGE HAPPINESS, CONFIDENCE, RESOURCEFULNESS

Brings joy to our workday and strengthens our appetite for life! Orange is the best emotional stimulant. It connects us to our senses and helps to remove inhibitions and makes us independent and social.

Personality Traits: Enthusiastic, happy, sociable, energetic, sporty, self-assured, and constructive.

The Spleen Chakra is governed by the orange energy

Crystals / Stones: Carnelian, coral and golden calcite

Scents: Sandalwood, gardenia and citrus

The Archangel: Gabriel

YELLOW WISDOM, CLARITY, SELF-ESTEEM

Gives us clarity of thought, increases awareness, and stimulates interest and curiosity. Yellow energy is related to the ability to perceive and understand. The yellow energy connects us to our mental self.

Personality Traits: Good-humored, optimistic, confident, practical, and intellectual.

The Solar Plexus Chakra is governed by the yellow energy

Crystals / Stones: Tiger eye, topaz, citrine, yellow sapphire, and Amber

Scents: Lemon and rosemary

The Archangel: Michael

GREEN BALANCE, LOVE, SELF CONTROL

Helps relax muscles, nerves, and thoughts. Cleanses and balances our energy, to give a feeling of renewal, peace, and harmony. Green connects us to unconditional love and is used for balancing our whole being.

Personality Traits: Understanding, self-control, adaptable, sympathetic, compassionate, generous, humble, nature loving, and romantic.

The Heart Chakra is governed by the green energy.

Crystals/ Stones: Green jade, emerald, kunzite, green tourmaline, moldavite and malachite

Scents: Rose oil and marjoram

The Archangel: Raphael

BLUE KNOWLEDGE, HEALTH, DECISIVENESS

This is a mentally relaxing color. Blue has a pacifying effect on the nervous system and brings great relaxation. Ideal for sleep problems and hyperactive children. Connects us to holistic thought and gives us wisdom and clarity enhancing communication and speech.

Personality Traits: Loyal, tactful, affectionate, inspiring, inventive, caring, and cautious.

The Throat Chakra is governed by the blue energy.

Crystals / Stones: Turquoise, aquamarine and danburite

Scents: Eucalyptus and frankincense

The Archangel: Kamael-Tzadkiel

INDIGO   INTUITION, MYSTICISM, UNDERSTANDING

The indigo energy connects us to our unconscious self and gives us the experience of being part of the whole universe. Strengthens intuition, imagination, psychic powers, and increases dream activity.

Personality Traits: Intuitive, fearless, practical, idealistic, wise, and a truth seeker.

The Brow Chakra is governed by the indigo energy.

Crystals / Stones: Lapis, lazuli, sodalite, and blue sapphire

Scents: Star Anise

The Archangel: Urial

VIOLET   BEAUTY, CREATIVITY, INSPIRATION

Purifies our thoughts and feelings giving us inspiration in all undertakings. The violet energy connects us to our spiritual self, bringing guidance, wisdom, and inner strength. Enhances artistic talent and creativity.

Personality Traits: Inspirational leaders, kindly and just, humanitarians, self-sacrificing, visionary, creative, and strong mentally.

The Crown Chakra is governed by the violet energy

Crystals / Stones: Amethyst, alexandrite, diamond, selenite and sugalite

Scents: Lotus and lavender

The Archangel: Metratron

Essential Oils: Can be used in diffusers, in a bath, body misters, room sprays or applied diluted on your skin.

Crystals / Gemstones: Will radiate energy to you. Put them in your bath, in your pocket or purse, on your desk or hold them when you meditate.

Food and Drink: Eat a rainbow selection of foods and you will find yourself eating better and feeling better. Drink cranberry, tomato or beet juice to kick start your day with some red vitality. Drink grapefruit or lemon juice to stimulate the digestive system with yellow energy.

Herbs: St. John Wort, an orange energy, is used for depression; and chamomile, a blue energy, is a relaxing and calming. Each herb has the healing power connected to a color and chakra.

Clothing: Pick your clothing colors according to what you want to experience that day. Socks and underwear are a great way of wearing colors you avoid because of a dislike or because of fashion constraints.

Interior Design: At home or work create the energy needed in each room, which suits the purpose or function of the room, through the decor of the walls, furniture, and accessories.

Solarized water: Place a colored glass filled with water in the sunlight. The sunlight amplifies the color energy into the water giving you its energy.

Sunlight: Has all the colors! Enjoy the sun everyday, even when it's cloudy you will still get the benefits.

Music: Notes are colors and can stimulate your body into moving (drumming sounds) versus some music can be sedating and calming (nature sounds).

Breathing, visualizing colors, dance, and sound are other ways to get color.

COLORS AND THEIR IMPACT ON OUR LIVES

DRESS IN RED WHEN YOU WISH:

- To express lots of energy and force
- To be seen
- To strengthen your sexual side
- To strengthen yourself sexually
- Wear in party attire - if you are not afraid of being approached or flirted with at sporting events - it shows strength, power, and endurance

DRESS IN ORANGE WHEN YOU WISH:
- ‿ To motivate yourself
- ‿ To react impulsively and let your emotions dictate your decisions
- ‿ To get in contact with more people
- ‿ To have fun and make others and yourself happy

DRESS IN YELLOW WHEN YOU WISH:
- ‿ To tell who you are and what you are capable of doing
- ‿ To stimulate yourself mentally
- ‿ To prevent depression
- ‿ To show that you can do more than just the multiplication table, very intellectual person
- ‿ Wear this when applying for a librarian or teacher position it radiates knowledge
- ‿ Also good for architects, bookkeepers, computer analysts, office clerks, engineers and technical writers.

DRESS IN GREEN WHEN YOU WISH:
- ‿ To ease headaches
- ‿ To be kind and good
- ‿ To give peace and balance to yourself and others
- ‿ To be for other people what you wish people would be for you
- ‿ Wear this when applying for nursing, counseling, childcare, secretarial, social work, florists, veterinarian, real estate agents, healers, or holistic positions.

DRESS IN BLUE WHEN YOU WISH:
- ‿ To show you are a wise, good, and spirited person
- ‿ To decrease hyperactivity
- ‿ To strengthen your analytical and logical side
- ‿ To show you have control over yourself and your surroundings
- ‿ To project an image of intelligence and self-control
- ‿ Wear when applying for a job in a bank — it gives impression of efficiency, order, and peace

ભ Also good for positions in ministry, missionary work, political realms, corporate heads, or management.

DRESS IN INDIGO WHEN YOU WISH:

ભ To stimulate your intuitive side

ભ To trust your feelings

ભ To calm your inner confusion

ભ To show that you have a mystical and mysterious side

ભ To be true to both yourself and mankind

ભ To work towards a higher goal and good for all concerned

ભ Wear this when applying for a creative position - this is a positive, inquisitive color

ભ Also this color is good for musicians, writers, designers, composers, clairvoyants, counselors, artists,

ભ Wear this when applying in theatre, television, and films and you believe your message can benefit the world

DRESS IN VIOLET WHEN YOU WISH:

ભ To be more secure about what you believe in

ભ To be an ambassador for the violet energy

ભ To feel inspired and surrounded by helpers

ભ To be attracted to all beautiful things that have life-energy

ભ To be connected to the emotional and spiritual realms of the universe

COLORS AND THEIR IMPACT INSIDE YOUR HOME

ભ VIBRANT COLORS like red, yellow, and bright blue make a ROOM SMALLER

ભ BRIGHT AND All PASTEL COLORS make a room seem LIGHTER and BIGGER

ભ WARM COLORS such as Red, Yellow, and Orange combined with wooden furniture give a WARM ATMOSPHERE

ભ ROMANTIC, COMPASSIONATE FEELING: all pink /rose colors

ભ SENSUAL FEELING: wine colors or burgundy

- ENHANCES FEELINGS OVERALL: peach, apricot, and salmon red
- HAPPINESS AND CHEERFULNESS: yellow, honey yellow or sun yellow
- CLARITY AND OPEN COMMUNICATION: turquoise, light blue, and azure
- ENHANCES DREAMS AND VISUALIZATION: dark blue
- REFRESHING FEELING & GOOD FOR HEALTH AND STABILITY: green, forest green, and emerald green.
- RELAXING, CALMING FEELING: sea green and mint green
- PEACEFUL FEELING AND FRESH THOUGHTS: blue/green, teal, and ocean blue
- ENHANCES SPIRITUALITY AND KNOWLEDGE: Purple
- Too much WHITE in a home will make it seem TOO COLD AND STARK
- Too much BLACK in a home will make it feel EMPTY AND TRANSITIONAL

VISUALIZATION EXERCISE

Close your eyes and see with your mind a beautiful rose. Imagine it opened and soft. See it, feel it, and/or smell it. Can you feel it in different areas of your body? What feeling does it give you? You can use your senses to learn how color and scents affect you. Often we are so busy in life, we aren't aware of how things affect us. We might remember how we slept poorly, but not take into account what we did to over stimulate ourselves. For instance a cup of cinnamon tea (which is a red energy), sleeping in a red nightie, watching a scary movie (which gets your adrenaline going) or listening to energizing red music just before bedtime, will affect your sleep and energy level the next day. Another example is trying to get work done while being surrounded by green walls, clothes and music and feeling unmotivated. There are many shades of each color, which blend into the next color. When we look at a rainbow we see how the colors flow into each other. Sometimes we will experience more of the red in orange and sometimes more of the yellow in it. Similarly with the scents, they can be more than one color and at different times you will experience them differently. For example, the most versatile essential oil, lavender, can calm you down or energize you according to how you feel and how much you use. Color is one of the easiest tools we have to help us with health, harmony, and balance. The more often we use color with awareness, the more often we can more fully experience what we want to experience in life.

BREATHING EXERCISE

Breath is our life force! Most people forget to breathe deeply and fully. When we breathe in air it also contains light, color, sound, aroma, and electro-magnetic energy. We breathe in the color vibration of the people, places, and objects around us. It is helpful to visualize yourself breathing in the colors you want and breathing out the colors (from pollution, other people's smoking, or depression) that you don't want.

Direct your color breathe in to any part of your body. The more intentionally you breathe color into yourself and your environment, the more you will experience the benefits. Say affirmations such as *"I breathe in the joys of life with orange," "I breathe in relaxation and calmness with blue,"* or *"I breathe in passion for life with red."* Imagine the red energy building in your root chakra and then drawing it up into your throat chakra for expressing your passion for life. Add aromatherapy, and you increase the vibration even more.

WHICH COLORS DO YOU RESONATE WITH AND IN WHICH PRIORITY?

Below there are seven questions. Each is matched to a different color energy. The purpose of this questionnaire is to help you become aware of where you are focusing your energies. Imbalances exist because we sometimes put more emphasis on what we consider the most important, neglecting areas which we consider to be of lesser value. You may find it more beneficial for you to focus on the areas you have ignored.

Answer these questions below by assigning a numerical value to each, with one being the most important to you and seven being the least.

A. YOUR PHYSICAL SELF: _____
    Your physical challenges and goals. Your body and sexual en-
    ergy. Sensory awareness: what you see, touch, smell, taste, and
    hear.

B. YOUR RELATIONSHIPS: _____
    Your need to interact with people, socializing and meeting
    new people and needing to have successful relationships.

C. USING YOUR INTELLECT: _____
    Needing to be challenged by mental studies and work. Your
    commitment to cooperation.

D. FINANCIAL SITUATION:_____
    Wanting or needing financial security in your life and family.
    Enjoyment in making others feel happy and secure. Your love
    of hearth and home.

E. PEACE AND ORDER:_____
    Ability to organize and plan. To see the big picture and plan
    accordingly. Your appreciation for beauty in your environ-
    ment.

F. UNDERSTANDING NEW THINGS: _____
    Your belief in your own inner strength and power to guide you
    through your challenges. Envisioning your future. Your confi-
    dence and ability to handle new situations.

G. CREATIVITY:_____
    Your ability to express yourself creatively and to generate
    ideas and express them effectively through music, art, or other
    creative pursuits. Your ability to be inspired by a higher power,
    and to be spiritually motivated.
    A- Red, B - Orange, C - Yellow, D - Green, E - Blue,
    F - Indigo, G - Violet
After you have answered the questions, check to see which are your

lowest color priorities and refer to these colors in the Color Energy book, booklets or reference charts. You will find that you can benefit from developing the qualities of the colors that are your lowest priority. As well note the color energy, which you listed as most important. Are you achieving this? If not, you may need to work on this color as well.

Sometimes working with a stimulating energy in the morning is the best way to start your day with some color power. In the evening it is better to work with the more calming color elements. For example, kick start your day by taking a red, orange, or yellow bath or doing a foot bath in color while taking your morning shower. Add a few drops of a correlating aromatherapy oil. Envision the power of this vibrant energy moving up your legs and into the chakra center that it is related to. Say out loud or in your mind what you want to bring in from that energy, such as *"I bring in red fire to motivate me to accomplish my goals and give me the courage and confidence to face any situation that arises in today."* When unplugging the drain, release any negative thoughts connected to that energy, letting go of any unneeded programs. Following this ritual, listen to energizing music. Drink a cup of power juice of that energy. At the end of the day, you can work with any of the calming energies to relax. Play with the different ways that you best bring in the different colors. Now isn't this a great way to start and end each day? If you do these simple exercises, you will find that you will feel more alive and have more color power to help you accomplish anything.

It is helpful for you to understand which energies you are using the most as well as the least. With knowing this information you can learn how you can bring every energy up to its fullest potential, thereby, consciously creating what you want instead of what you don't want. The Color Energy Test is a great tool for finding out where you are and what tools you can use to enhance the quality of your life. It also makes a great gift to ourselves and to others as what we are all striving for is to know ourselves, be ourselves, and express ourselves. May you find the many gifts that you have. And may you share the joy to express and the joy to give and receive, so you can create harmony and balance!

FYI: 45.3% of North America's population is strongest in their yellow left brain and mental intelligence. The Violet visionary intelligence is next at 13.7%. Statistically the Red's body intelligence is last at 2.75%. This means that we are governed by our mind power and place little emphasis on our body's health and well being! What colour are you?

Colour Energy Corporation is the world leader in offering a complete line of chakra therapy products. If you would love to try their wonderful color bath treatments, or have your color personality analyzed, please fill out the form in the back of the book and we would be glad to send them to you.

Recommended Reading:
Colour Energy book written by Inger Naess
The Rainbow Guide To Color Energy by Cynthia Whitehouse

Chapter Five

Crystals and Gemstones
How They Can Impact Your Life

So much has been written about crystals that sometimes the information can be overwhelming. When choosing a rock, one of the first things people do is look in a book or ask someone else about its properties. So often what a book or person says will influence our decision. If we listened to our own guidance and used our intuition, the stone we need would come home with us.

Here are some suggestions that may work for you when choosing a stone:

- ❧ Before entering a place to purchase your stone, center and ground yourself.
- ❧ Check in with your body and see how it feels.
- ❧ After entering the place, stop for a moment and see what direction your body is telling you to go.
- ❧ Keep checking in with yourself and go with the flow.
- ❧ The stone will be directing and calling you to it.
- ❧ When you come to the stone that has drawn you, take time to ask your body how it feels. Center and ground yourself again.
- ❧ Pick up the stone and ask it, "Are you the one for me?"
- ❧ Try hard not to ask or look in a book about the stone.

The next part is seeing what the stone or crystal does for you. While holding the stone, feel where in your body the energy goes. Does it go to your heart chakra, the solar plexus area? Does the stone make you happy, peaceful, and light or do you soar? The most important part is to keep yourself grounded, centered, and conscious of your body.

Here are some suggestions on what may work when sensing what the stone does for you:

- ◌ Take a moment to center and ground yourself.
- ◌ Pick up the stone and pay attention to how the stone makes you feel.
- ◌ See where the energy of the stone goes in your body.
- ◌ What effect it has on your body is the most important.
- ◌ Try hard not to ask anyone else about the stone properties.

Often times people allow what is written about a stone's properties to limit or influence what that stone may do for them. Let's use rose quartz as an example. You are drawn to that stone, which people say equates to love. You pick it up and think, "This stone is used for love." You never allow yourself to explore the other possibilities of this mineral. You can only imagine that it is a "stone of love." Thus, it is possible that you never really sense all that the rose quartz has to offer simply because you allowed another's input to limit your experience.

Certainly, books are a great source of information and have their place. Unfortunately, too often we use that resource to direct our choices instead of using the most valuable resource we have, our intuition. Another issue to consider when reading about stones is the region from which your stone originates. For instance, a stone you are considering buying is from India, but the book you are reading may be discussing a stone from Utah. You will find that a stone's properties will differ because of the influence of its origin.

Once you have chosen your stone and brought it home, you will want to bless and cleanse it. Intention is key here. Take time when you first bring a stone into your home to say a blessing over the stone. For the blessing, you may want to pick a prayer or something that is true for you. There are many ways to cleanse a stone. You may put it in the light of the new or full moon, soak it in saltwater, bury it in the earth or rinse it with spring water and allow the sun to dry it. Try different methods and see which feels right for you. With all of these, intention is the most important element.

Here are some suggestions on what may work when cleaning your stones:

- ∝ Choose which cleansing method feels right for you.
- ∝ Center and ground yourself.
- ∝ Set your intentions for the highest good.
- ∝ Cleanse your stone.
- ∝ When finished, check in with your stone and see how it feels.

Your stone will need to be cleansed throughout its life with you. You will sense when it needs to be cleaned. Does it feel sluggish, low-energy or simply "dirty?" Always check in with your stone about cleaning and they will inform you.

MEDITATION WITH STONES

Stones can transmit a lot of information and facilitate with your meditation. They can allow you to go deeper in meditation because of their calming energies and can also bring messages to you from other times and dimensions. There are many ways to use them in meditation.

Here are some suggestions on what may work when using them in meditation:

- ∝ Choose the stone or stones with which you would like to meditate.
- ∝ Center and ground yourself.
- ∝ Place the stone in front of you so you can focus on it visually; hold the stone in your hand, or place it on your body while meditating.
- ∝ Stones can also be placed around the room to "hold space" for your meditation.
- ∝ Enjoy your stones during meditation whether they help you go deeper, bring you messages, or simply share your space.

Remember not to set any expectations. The stone and meditation will take you on a wonderful ride.

HEALING WITH STONES

Stones are brought to us for many reasons; meditation is just one of those. They also are wonderful healing facilitators. Some stones may come into your life for healing purposes. If so, allow the stone's energies to help where there is need. Do not put limitations by thinking it does only one thing. Remember the information contained in books is just general guidance. Do not allow yourself to limit what the stone can do. Keep an open mind and let the energy flow where it is needed.

Here are some suggestions on what may work when using stones for healing:

- ଓ Before using for healing, always cleanse it.
- ଓ Center and ground yourself.
- ଓ Let your intuition guide you in stone placement.
- ଓ If the healing is for you, check in with your body and see how it feels.
- ଓ If healing another, discuss the stones you are using and ask them how it feels.
- ଓ Clear your mind and let the energy flow where needed.
- ଓ When finished, you always need to cleanse the stones used for healing. This is especially true before using them on another person.

Stones can hold energies, good and bad. It is important that between healings you cleanse the stones. If you do not, the energies picked up from the previous healing can be transmitted to the next person.

USING STONES FOR PROTECTING YOUR SPACE

Using stones for healing the body is one way of healing, but you can also use the stone for healing your space or environment. Different stones can be used for the protection of your home, workspace, and yard. You can set up grids for protecting your space. You can also use the stones for setting a particular type of energy you would like in your workspace. If you are feeling negativity or hostility or the space is just unpleasant, bring a few stones to work. Placing them in various spots around the office can change the environment. The addition of a water source, such as a small fountain, to absorb the negativity will allow the stones to transform the energy of the room. If you cannot have a water source in your work environment, the stones can cleanse and transform the energies. You will just need to take them home and cleanse them more often. Once again, it is important that the intention be for the highest good. If the stone are used for any other purpose, the effect will not be the same.

Here are some suggestions on what may work when using stones for the work place:

  ೞ Center and ground yourself.
  ೞ Pick the stones that would help with the environment. If unsure, ask the stones or check with your intuition or your body for the answer.
  ೞ Set the intention for the highest good.
  ೞ When placing the stone or stones, ask for guidance.
  ೞ After introducing the stones, bless the space.

Before placing the stones in the workspace, take note of the energies in this space. After placing the stones about the room, pay attention to the feeling of the space. Watch for the energy shifts from that day forward. As time passes, feel the difference in the room. Pay attention to how the people entering the room react. Remember that occasionally you will need to cleanse the stones in this room.

You may also want to set a grid of protection around your home. You will need to choose the stones for this task and place a stone at each corner of the house. Maybe you want to put a grid of protection over your home or set the energy in a certain room to be different than that of other rooms. All of this can be done. You can pick a stone and set a single intention for that stone as long as it is for the highest good. If you desire to set a grid for your home to keep your house safe and protected, that is the intention to set and the stones will do just that.

Here are some suggestions on what may work when using stones in your home or setting a grid around your home:

- ∞ Center and ground yourself.
- ∞ Pick the stones that will help with the environment. If unsure, ask the stones or check with your intuition or your body for the answer.
- ∞ Set the intention either for the highest good or be specific about what you desire the stone to accomplish, as long as it is for the highest good.
- ∞ If setting a grid outside, dig four holes at the corners of your home. Place the stones in these holes and cover them with soil.
- ∞ If setting a grid within your home, place stones in the four corners of the space.
- ∞ You can also have just one stone for a room. In this case, seek guidance from your intuition where it is to be placed.
- ∞ After putting the stones in place, bless the space and ask for divine protection.

Stones that have been placed in the home will need to be cleansed on occasion. The stones placed around the outside of your home can remain in place and never be touched again. The earth will take care of their cleaning. You will find that new stones will come into your life and replace the ones that are currently in your space. Look at it as a growing experience. The newcomers have something to teach or to help you.

Stones come into your life for many reasons. They bring beauty, warmth, life, stories, and love. It is a way for us to have a connection with this beautiful Mother Earth. To have stones in our space is to have access to parts of the world we may never see in person. With a touch, you can feel the vibration and possibly travel to where we may never go in person. Stones can heal our bodies, mind, and spirit. All it takes is an open mind and belief. If we set our intention for the highest good, bring ourselves into the present moment, and allow ourselves the opportunity to grow and learn, anything can happen.

One thing that has been mentioned in this chapter is not to let reading material influence what a stone can do for you. This is simply my opinion. It is important to read all you can so you can learn and form your own opinion. There are many different healing, cleansing and meditation methods available to you through reading. It is critical you do not just rely on the books. Do not use them as your only source of information. You have the best source of all; your intuition will tell what needs to be in your life. If you do not set limitations on what the stones can do for you, there are no limits on where they can lead you. Remember: ground and center yourself, set your intentions, say a blessing, and let the stones come to you. The world and its stones can be your playground.

CRYSTALS AND GEMSTONES

Crystals and gemstones have captivated human interest for centuries. They have been used in cultures throughout the ages for adornment, used in healing practices, as well as in art. Throughout history, gemstones and crystals played a part in culture. Certain stones were used to adorn crowns, scepters, and swords. Royalty and noblemen used crystals and gemstones to show their wealth.

Crystals and gemstones still hold their mystical power over us today. Crystals generate a vibration of their own. Color may first attract you or the shape or size may catch your eye. Yet certain crystals and gemstones seem to reach out to you on a different level. It is something you cannot seem to explain. It is believed that the healing properties of these stones aid in the balancing of emotions. They can promote an overall well being of the person using the crystal. Various stones are used during meditation. Many still use crystals and gemstones as talismans. Pendulums are made from different types of stones. Even decorative water fountains are made out of various crystals. Large gems make beautiful bookends.

Crystals and gemstones can be used during massages. Crystals can be used on acupuncture, acupressure, and reflexology points. Stones are used to help balance our chakras.

Crystals and gemstones captivate us with their beauty. Twelve gemstones symbolize the month we were born, called birthstones. Jewelry is made using numerous crystal and gemstones. Wearing crystal pendants or placing it on a key ring allows the individual to have that stone with them at all times.

Here is a list of popular crystals and gemstones and some of their known qualities:

Amazonite   Helps one to speak the truth and communicate clearly. Promotes sincerity, trust, clarity and expression of your personal truth.

Amethyst   Brings inner peace, spiritual awareness, and Divine Connection. Used for protection and in meditation. Helps with breaking bad habits. Promotes balance and healing. Releases mystic, spiritual, and psychic wisdom.

Aquamarine Stone of courage and strength, it calms fears and releases what is no longer needed. It brings serenity, inspiration, tranquility, peace, and cleansing.

Aventurine Enhances success, prosperity, and growth and is used for good luck. It heals the heart and emotions, bringing blessings of health, wealth, and happiness.

Azurite   Awakens the third eye. It assists in positive transformation, clear understanding, perspective, insight, and kindness and develops intuition.

Bloodstone Balances emotions. It is used to calm, ground, revitalize, smooth energy flow, idealism, and purification. It can provide courage to recognize the path your heart is leading you.

Blue Lace Agate Promotes patience and peace, helping to lessen stress. It is considered a general healer.

Carnelian   Encourages individuality, emotional warmth, self-esteem, happiness and assists in taking action in your life.

Chrysocolla Communicate your heart to others. It resonates to hope, honesty, intimacy, peace, and serenity.

Citrine   Vibrates to the second and third chakras, releasing creative energy. It brings comfort, warmth and career success and helps with mental and emotional clarity.

Clear Quartz Encourages protection, harmony of the body and mind,

	allowing clear thinking, positive thoughts.
Emerald	Stone of successful love, domestic bliss, joy, and harmony.
Fluorite	Stone for concentration, grounding, and self-discipline. It helps one to think objectively and impartially and offers psychic protection and healing. It is an important balancer.
Garnet	Stone of fertility, abundance, and prosperity. It repels negative energy and stimulates the Kundalini flow.
Hematite	Encourages concentration, reliability, optimism, and willpower. It helps break free of self-imposed limitations.
Jade	Promotes health, wealth, longevity, practical wisdom, tranquility, and balance.
Jasper	Enhances relaxation. It is a supreme nurturer, providing grounding.
Kunzite	Promotes Divine love and joy, gentleness, friendliness, self-love, and unconditional love. It opens the emotional and spiritual heart.
Kyanite	Aligns all chakras automatically, Facilitating meditation and dream recall.
Labradorite	Strengthens and protects aura. It opens energy flow to centers most in need and helps us relate to others.
Lapis Lazuli	Stone of total awareness, inner power, and self-confidence. It is used to enhance one's ability to learn and comprehend.
Lepidolite	Calms and relaxes. It promotes cosmic awareness, acceptance, emotional balance, faith, and prayer.
Malachite	Helps clear influences of the ego from the will. It clears emotional blocks and draws out negativity.
Moonstone	Energy relates to new beginnings, enhancing the intuitive and receptive side of the mind.
Obsidian	Promotes inner growth, positive change, and fulfillment. It is the stone of protection.
Onyx	Enhances self-control and mental clarity. It balances and grounds.
Pyrite	Used for focus, practicality and logic, providing grounding.

Rose Quartz Stone of Unconditional Love. It enhances all forms of
love and promotes forgiveness.

Ruby   Associated with enthusiasm, happiness, passion, and
romance.

Smokey Quartz Very grounding, it ddissolves negative energy and
provides protection.

Sodalite   Enables us to gain access to the Akashic records
(library where every person's path is recorded and
stored.) It stabilizes mental and emotional processes
and provides direction.

Tigers Eye   Ability to see clearly without illusions.

Tourmaline   Strengthens body and spirit. It enhances objectivity
and inner peace. (Black: protection; Blue: peace;
Green: prosperity; Pink: love.

Turquoise   Stone of vision. It promotes honest communication
and emotional sensitivity and brings wisdom.

Zircon (Clear)   Purification, truth and intuition.

This list is just a sampling of the vast amount of crystals and gemstones that are available.

Recommended Reading:
Gems a Lively Guide for the Casual Collector by Daniel J. Dennis Jr.
Crystal Wisdom by Dolfyn
The Crystal Ally Cards, The Crystal Path to Self Knowledge
   by Naisha Ahsian
Crystal Acupuncture by Margaret Rogers
Love Is In The Earth: A Kaleidoscope Of Crystals, by Melody
The Women's Book Of Healing, by Diane Stein

Chapter Six

Color Candles Their Meanings And How To Use Them

There is no historical record of the first candles used by man, however clay candleholders dating back to the 4th century BC have been found in Egypt. The first candle known in America dates to the first century AD. Candle making as we know it began in the 13th century when traveling candlers went door to door making dipped tapers from their clients beeswax.

Candles are used to set the mood or ambiance of a room. They are used to light a room in the dark. Candles are flexible in use, they can be used from almost any tradition or religious purpose, including birthdays, to just being a pretty decoration in a room. Candles come in various shapes, sizes, and colors, such as pillar, taper, votive, 7-day glass enclosed candles, and tea lights to name a few. Some candles are scented and others have no scent at all. Candles burn for a few minutes, several hours, or even days when using a novena or 7-day candle.

When using candles for meditation or prayer time, they not only set the mood, but staring into the flame can calm the individual and help to relax, focus, and enter Into a deeper state of meditation. When putting a candle out it is best to use a candlesnuffer. It is believed that blowing a candle out takes away from your prayers or intentions you placed when lighting the candle. Trim wicks prior to each use. If burning a Novena candle for days, be certain that you have a place where you can leave it burning safely. Perhaps place it in a metal pie or cake pan. This is in case the glass should crack (which seldom occurs, yet it is a preventative measure). This way the wax will spill into the pan and not on your table or counter, and is less likely to catch fire.

TYPE OF CANDLES:

Aromatherapy Candles — These candles use oils from flowers, plants and herbs, as well as fruits. Essential oils are used that assist in various therapeutic benefits.

The 7 Knobbed Candle — this candle has seven knobs or bumps. Burn one knob each day while praying, making a wish, or special intentions.

Novena Candles — The word "novena" is Latin, meaning a new beginning. The idea is to burn away your old troubles, or mistakes and begin anew with a clean unobstructed viewpoint. These candles come in 3, 7, 9 or 14- day and are glass enclosed. Some are decorated with pictures, symbols, and even prayers. Once lit, you need to let them burn all the way down, without blowing them out.

Triple Colored Candles — Triple action candles are another way to cleanse an environment or people of negative influences. It is believed that these candles release the highest spiritual vibration, banishing the negative influences. These candles are often burned to bring good luck into the home. The more popular are red, white, and blue, that symbolize "Health, Purity, and Peace," or red, white, and green, that symbolizes "Health, Peace, and Prosperity."

Spectrum Candles — a glass enclosed candle, with seven different colors layered on top of one another. These candles cover all bases, needs and wishes.

Color Candles – Color candles enhance the mood and ambiance. Each color has its own vibration and purpose.

Black	Changes in luck, either good or bad, release or negativity, unexpected happenings
White	Purity, truth, spiritual strength, power, realization, holy spirit/angels/spirit guides
Turquoise	Communication, confidence, oratory, strength, concentration, free expression.

Red	Passion, vitality, courage, strength, self-confidence, love security, will-power, love and relationships
Pink	Unconditional love, friendships, consideration, kindness, unselfishness, modesty, removes unwanted aggression and irritation, protects, gives peace of mind.
Orange	Confidence, happiness, resourcefulness, health, joy, physical actions and activity of all kinds.
Gold	Understanding, great fortune, and fast luck.
Yellow	Clarity, wisdom, self-esteem, intellect, awareness, curiousity, stimulates interest, relocation for work, passing test, moving in general.
Green	Prosperity, balance, self-control, harmony, money, success, jobs, family, children, and birth. Also relaxes muscles and thoughts.
Blue	Knowledge, health and recovery, communication, inspiration, devotion, loyalty, mental relaxation, enhances speech and communication.
Purple	Inspiration, meditation, authority, creativity, spirituality, enhances artistic talent.
Indigo	Intuition, deep meditation, understanding, increases dream activity and remembrance.

Some like to associate a certain color candle with a day of the week, a month or a season.

Sunday – Gold or White
Monday – Silver or Pink
Tuesday – Red or Pink
Wednesday – Yellow or Purple
Thursday – Bright Blue
Friday – Emerald Green or Light Green
Saturday – Purple or Black

Spring – Green
Summer – Red
Autumn – Yellow
Winter – Blue
January – Garnet or Red

February – Navy Blue
March – Pink
April – White
May – Navy Blue
June – Light Blue
July – Dark Green or Emerald Green
August – Light Green
September – Gold
October – Red
November – Brown
December – Dark Green or Emerald Green

To help you prepare, find a quiet room and close your eyes and relax. Visualize all negative thoughts, energies and feelings leaving the room and the room getting filled with beautiful white light. Make sure you clear all corners, nook and crannies and allow the white light to fill your room completely with universal truth, love and consciousness. Slowly open your eyes and say aloud: *"All ill and negativity has been banished and removed from this room and my life and positive vibes instilled. As I say it, so it is! Amen!!"*

You can write your dreams and wished down on a piece of paper and place it underneath your candle. Be very specific and direct. Be careful what you wish for; you may just get it!! Now light your candle and picture your need, wish or dream. All you need is to believe that lighting your candle will help. For example, if you need more money, then visualize all of your bills paid, money for new clothes, money for a well-needed vacation. Don't focus on HOW or WHERE the money will come, just that it will. Picture the bills paid, yourself in new clothes or on a vacation. Focus on that vision, wish or dream and allow the candle to burn freely. It is all right to put a candle out and relight it later. It is better to use a snuffer then to blow it out. Every time you relight your candle, picture your need and repeat this exercise. After doing this exercise, watch for coincidences, signs or events that take place in the coming days or weeks that let you see your wish is being fulfilled.

Here are some simple prayers or sayings to say while lighting candles:

Mother/Father God, Angels, Master, Spirit Guides above of the
white light, I ask for your presence this evening.
As I light this candle,
I ask for your guidance and wisdom. I ask that you hear my wishes,
dreams and request that I have with me tonight and
I ask that you help me to fulfill them.
AMEN

Please feel free to adjust it to make it comfortable for you, your beliefs and needs.

CANDLE EXERCISE TO BALANCE THE CHAKRAS

Starting with the 1st chakra, place a red floater candle in a glass bowl filled with water, light the floater. Sit quietly. As you find that peaceful place within, bring your awareness to the 1st chakra. Visualize it as a red wheeling spinning clockwise. Breathe in this red color, and breathe out the old stagnant energy color, which is thought of as gray. Do this for several breaths until the color of your out-breath matches the color of your in-breath.

Then repeat the related chakra affirmation as a mantra. As you feel complete, extinguish the chakra floater with a candlesnuffer. Repeat the above exercise with each chakra using the appropriate chakra floater, color and affirmation. Never leave lit candles unattended. Tea lights candles are great for this exercise.

7th CHAKRA AFFIRMATION: (red candle) I allow myself to become one with the divine energy that connects us all for true balance.

6th CHAKRA AFFIRMATION: (orange candle) I open myself to the inner vision, which brings understanding of my spiritual truths.

5th CHAKRA AFFIRMATION: (yellow candle) I express myself freely and openly knowing that I am seen and heard just as I desire to be.

4th CHAKRA AFFIRMATION: (green candle) I feel harmonious and compassionate toward myself and all around me, the pinnacle of love.

3rd CHAKRA AFFIRMATION: (blue candle) I free myself to the power of living my life to the fullest, feeling worthy of all that I receive.

2nd CHAKRA AFFIRMATION: (violet/lavender candle) I allow my sensuality to flow and achieve my most ambitious desires without sacrificing those I love and care for.

1st CHAKRA AFFIRMATION: (purple or white candle) I allow myself to be both physically safe and tranquil within my world.

Chapter Seven

Reiki - What is it and How Can I Use it?

Reiki (**ray-key**) is a technique that aids the body in releasing stress and tension by creating deep relaxation. Reiki is a technique that allows everyone to tap into an unlimited supply of *life force energy* to improve health and enhance the quality of life. Because of this, Reiki promotes healing and health. The word Reiki is made of two Japanese words: **Rei** which means "the Wisdom of God" or "the Higher Power" and **Ki** which means "life force energy." So Reiki means, "spiritually guided life force energy," which is channeled through the healer and received by the body of the recipient as gentle supportive healing energy.

Reiki is taught in three levels: Level 1, Level 2, and Master. **Level 1** attunes you to the energy to a level of 40 percent and allows you to work on yourself and others. **Level 2** attunes you the other 60 percent and also allows you to do long distance healings. **Master level** is a life-commitment to practice and teach others and help with global issues.

The Reiki system of healing is a technique for transmitting this subtle energy to yourself and others through the hands into the human energy system. Reiki restores energy balance and vitality by relieving the physical and emotional effects of unreleased stress. It gently and effectively opens blocked meridians and chakras and clears the energy bodies, leaving one feeling relaxed and at peace. Reiki treats the whole person including body, emotions, mind, and spirit and creates many beneficial effects including relaxation and feelings of peace, security, and well-being. Many have reported miraculous results. Reiki is a simple, natural, and safe method of spiritual healing and self-improvement that everyone can use.

Please know that the recipient of Reiki is always in control of the healing experience. There is no need to disrobe, ever. You may elect to be touched, as you see fit for your highest good. Reiki does not challenge nor conflict with any religious belief systems. Reiki may be used, if desired with all other treatment modalities, and will enhance the healing experience. Reiki does not diagnose, prescribe, nor cure. It addresses the energetic disturbance and balances the body in a state of relaxation allowing it to access its own innate wisdom, and thus, healing occurs.

Reiki is a powerful, precise system of healing which is believed to have originated in Tibet thousands of years ago. It accesses a Universal life force energy, and this energy also known as Prana, Mana, Chi, Holy Spirit, and Source. It helps promote healing in all living things on the physical, mental, emotional and spiritual levels.

IS REIKI A RELIGION?

While Reiki is spiritual in nature, it is not a religion. It has no dogma, and there is nothing you must believe in order to learn and use Reiki. In fact, Reiki is not dependent on belief at all and will work whether you believe in it or not.

REIKI CAN NEVER CAUSE HARM

Because the Divine or a Universal-consciousness guides Reiki, it can never do harm. It always knows what a person needs and will adjust itself to create the effect that is appropriate for them. The practitioner is just the vehicle for the healing and actually not doing the healing personally. The light force will go where it needs to go, no ego needed. This allows the Divine or Universal force to shine clearly through.

HOW IS A REIKI TREATMENT GIVEN?

In a standard treatment Reiki energy flows from the practitioner's hands into the client. The client is usually laying on a massage table but treatments can also be given while the client is seated or even standing. The client remains fully clothed. The practitioner places her/his hands on or near the client's body in a series of hand positions. These include positions around the head and shoulders, the stomach, and feet. Other, more specific positions may be used based on the client's needs. Each position is held for three to ten minutes depending on how much Reiki the client needs at each position. The whole treatment usually lasts between 45 and 90 minutes.

WHAT DOES A REIKI TREATMENT FEEL LIKE?

What one experiences during a Reiki treatment varies somewhat from person to person; many experience the warming effect of the reiki being transmitted into their body, almost like a warm hug. Feelings of deep relaxation and a new kind of peace are usually felt by all. As the Reiki energy encourages one to let go of all tension, anxiety, fear or other negative feelings a state of peace and well-being is experienced. Some drift off to sleep or report floating outside their bodies or have visions and other mystical experiences. At the end of the treatment, one feels refreshed with a more positive, balanced outlook.

HOW DOES REIKI HEAL?

Reiki restores energy balance and vitality by relieving the physical and emotional effects of unreleased stress. It gently and effectively opens blocked meridians and chakras and clears the energy bodies, leaving one feeling relaxed and at peace.

REIKI CAN:

- ೮ೠ Accelerate healing
- ೮ೠ Assist the body in cleansing toxins
- ೮ೠ Balance the flow of subtle energy by releasing blockages
- ೮ೠ Help the client contact the "healer within"
- ೮ೠ Treat the person's body, emotions, mind and spirit as a whole
- ೮ೠ An effective alternative or complement to massage therapy

ꝏ Supports any medical, or supplemental healing methods a client may be using

A treatment feels like warm, gentle sunshine, which flows through you, surrounds you, and comforts you. Reiki is a simple, natural and safe method of spiritual healing and self-improvement that everyone can use.

Reiki is powerful, yet wonderfully gentle and nurturing. It is gaining interest among chiropractors, medical doctors, physiotherapists, psycho- therapists, psychologists, and hypnotherapists. Anyone can learn to tap into an unlimited supply of "life force energy" to improve health and enhance the quality of life by learning Reiki or by receiving treatments from a Reiki Practitioner or Master.

WHAT CAN BE TREATED?

Reiki is both powerful and gentle. In its long history of use it has aided in healing virtually every known illness and injury including serious problems, such as multiple sclerosis, heart disease, and cancer as well as skin problems, cuts, bruises, broken bones, headache, colds, flu, sore throat, sunburn, fatigue, insomnia, impotence, poor memory, and even lack of confidence. It is always beneficial and works to improve the effectiveness of all other types of therapy. A treatment feels like a wonderful glowing radiance and has many benefits for both client and practitioner, including altered states of consciousness and spiritual experiences. If a client has a health condition and wants to be treated with Reiki, it is recommended that they do so under the supervision of an enlightened medical doctor or other health care professional. Reiki will improve the results of all medical treatment, acting to reduce negative side effects, shorten healing time, reduce or eliminate pain, reduce stress, and help create optimism.

DOES ONE HAVE TO STOP SEEING A REGULAR DOCTOR IN ORDER TO RECEIVE A REIKI TREATMENT?

Reiki works in conjunction with regular medical or psychological treatment. If one has a medical or psychological condition, it is recommended that one see a licensed health care professional in addition to receiving Reiki treatments. Reiki energy works in harmony with all other forms of healing, including drugs, surgery, psychological care or any other method of alternative care and will improve the results.

CAN ANYONE LEARN REIKI?

Yes, it is simply passed on from the teacher to the student, and it is easily learned in one weekend session. The ability to learn Reiki is not dependent on intellectual capacity, individual talent, or acquired ability, just a willingness to receive. As soon as this happens, one has and can do Reiki. The feeling of being connected directly to the Divine's healing love and protection is clearly apparent and very rewarding. Reiki is a very simple technique to learn and is not dependent on one having any prior experience with healing, meditation or any other kind of training. It has been successfully learned by over one million people from all walks of life, both young and old. The ability to do Reiki is simply transferred from the teacher to the student through a process called an attunement that takes place during a Reiki class. As soon as one receives an attunement, they have the ability to do Reiki and after that whenever one places their hands on themselves or on another person with the intention of doing Reiki, the healing energy will automatically begin flowing.

HOW LONG DOES IT TAKE TO LEARN REIKI?

A beginning Reiki class is taught on a weekend. The class can be one or two days long. I recommend that the minimum time necessary be at least six to seven hours. Along with the attunement, it is necessary that the student be shown how to give treatments and also to practice giving treatments in class.

WHAT IS THE ATTUNEMENT ?

Reiki is not taught in the way other healing techniques are taught. It is transferred to the student by the Reiki Master during an attunement process. This process opens the crown, heart, and palm chakras and creates a special link between the student and the Reiki source. The Reiki attunement is a powerful spiritual experience. The attunement energies are channeled into the student through the Reiki Master. The process is guided by the Rei or God-consciousness and makes adjustments in the process depending on the needs of each student. Many report having mystical experiences involving personal messages, healings, visions, and past life experiences. The attunement can also increase psychic sensitivity. Many have often reported experiences involving: opening of the third eye, increased intuitive awareness, and other psychic abilities after receiving a Reiki attunement.

Once you have received a Reiki attunement, you will have Reiki for the remainder of your life. It does not wear off and you can never lose it. One attunement is all you need for each level to be attuned to that level. The Reiki attunement can start a cleansing process that affects the physical body as well as the mind and emotions. Toxins that have been stored in the body may be released along with feelings and thought patterns that are no longer useful. Therefore, a process of purification prior to the attunement is recommended to improve the benefit one receives.

CAN I TREAT MYSELF?

Yes, once you have received the attunement, you can treat yourself as well as others. This is one of the unique features of Reiki.

QUESTIONS TO ASK ABOUT REIKI TRAINING

For yourself:

- ○8 Should I study Reiki at this time ?
- ○8 Do I feel in my heart that I should study with this person ?
- ○8 Will Reiki benefit me and my personal life journey ?
- ○8 Am I willing to commit to regular practice so that this method may yield results ?

For a Reiki teacher:

- ○8 What do you cover in your classes ?
- ○8 How many hours of class time is there ?
- ○8 How much time is instructional and how much is hands-on practice ?
- ○8 What should I expect from an attunement ?
- ○8 What are your fees ?

      ∞   How long should I wait between levels of Reiki training ?

      ∞   What is the availability for support from you or other Masters after I take this training ?

      ∞   Is there a Reiki support group in my area, or can you help me establish one ?

      ∞   Does the teacher respond in a loving manner that is supportive and empowering for you ?

GROWING WITH REIKI

Learning Reiki is a good starting point for experiencing and working with healing energy and a wonderful method for deepening awareness of universal energy. In general, Reiki complements other healing methods and spiritual practices. There are no hard and fast rules about how to approach starting Reiki and starting healing. Again, listen to your heart and you will be guided in choosing the right experiences and teachers for you.

Once you have learned a healing technique, the work begins. To develop your understanding and sensitivity, it is a good idea to devote time to regular practice, find a supportive teacher and practice group, and pursue continuing study. Make sure that you arrange circumstances so that you can be nurtured in your healing and growth.

Keep your eyes on your goals, your mind in your heart and take things one step at a time. Love and light to you in your journey.

The following ideals are both guidelines for living a gracious life and virtues worthy of practice for their inherent value.

The secret art of inviting happiness
The miraculous medicine of all diseases
Just for today, do not anger
Do not worry and be filled with gratitude
Devote yourself to your work. Be kind to people.
Every morning and evening, join your hands in prayer.
Pray these words to your heart
and chant these words with your mouth
Usui Reiki Treatment for the improvement of body and mind
           The founder, Usui Mikao

THE REIKI PRINCIPLES

Just for today, I will give thanks for my many blessings
Just for today, I will not worry
Just for today, I will not be angry
Just for today, I will do my work honestly
Just for today, I will be kind to my neighbor and every living thing.

ANOTHER VERSION OF THE REIKI PRINCIPLES

Just for today do not worry
Just for today do not anger
Honor your parents, teachers, and elders
Respect the oneness of all life
Show gratitude
Make your living honestly

Recommended books for further learning:
Essential Reiki – a Complete Guide To An Ancient Healing Art by
   Diane Stein
Reiki, the Healing Touch by William Lee Rand

The Reiki Handbook by Larry Arnold and Sandy Nevius

   If you would like to be trained in Reiki, please contact Acaysha about the schedule of classes. 888 759 5371 or acaysha@acaysha.com

Chapter Eight

Massage and Raindrop Therapy

Massage therapy has changed a lot over the centuries, and it is just that, therapy or the act of caring for someone. In the times of the Greeks and Romans, massage was used to help with injuries and muscle problems for soldiers returning from battle. Today, it is a means of helping someone regain and/or keep good health.

Massage has moved from something expected in red light districts and given by people of questionable cleanliness to a part of mainstream healthcare today. Licensed massage therapists are trained for hundreds of hours in anatomy, physiology, healthcare, disease, and several styles of massage. Their goal is to help the client regain a level of heath that they may have had before being injured, and also help people with no injuries maintain health simply by the beneficial effects massage has on the body. Another goal of massage therapists is to keep muscles toned for people that can't work their muscles properly or regularly.

The technical definition:

Massage is the systematic and scientific manipulation of the soft tissues of the body; administered to nude skin for the purpose of promoting and maintaining healthy body function.

In non-technical lay-man language:
Massage is where the skin and muscles are pulled, pushed, and generally rubbed.

This manipulation is done to get various physiological functions to go to work. These functions improve blood flow to help healing and clean wastes from the body. Massage also has a calming effect to help a person relax. Oil or lotion is generally used to cut down on friction so the movements of massage feels good instead of hurting.

Generally for a massage, the client is asked to undress to their comfort level. Although the ideal situation is for the client to be completely undressed, some people are not comfortable with this and will leave on underwear. Keep in mind that you can leave on whatever clothing makes you feel comfortable, but unless you remain completely clothed, the therapist will be using oil or lotion, and they don't want to get that on your clothing. In proper massage the client is covered or draped at all times with either a sheet or a towel. At no time should the genitals or breasts of women be exposed. During a normal session, the full body is slowly worked, including the entire back side of the body and the front, except for genitals and breasts (women only). This is *always* at the discretion, and within the comfort levels of the subject. If ever you feel uncomfortable with what a therapist is doing, tell them, and they will change it. Massage from a licensed professional *is not sexual* — **Massage is healthcare**.

For the most part, a massage is scheduled as a one-hour session. Other session lengths can be scheduled from 30 minutes up to two hours. An hour is generally a good time period. Thirty minutes usually feels too short. Longer than an hour can be done, depending on the client's ability to lie on a table and the amount of muscle work needed. Some people have problems that prevent them from lying still for very long. You just need to choose what feels best for you and meets your personal needs. Although massage most commonly follows the definition above, there are many types and styles of the art.

TYPES OF MASSAGES AVAILABLE
Swedish massage — Is the most common style of massage. This was based on movements observed in Swedish gymnastics. This style

uses a lot of long strokes, kneading, and a little percussion. It is a nice relaxing time. Although a Swedish massage is mostly for relaxation and maintaining good health, problem areas can be worked making the session therapeutic, and helping to correct problems such as muscle pulls, sore backs, and stiffness. Deep work can be used as needed to address all problems until they are better. Also, the pressure can be changed based on the comfort of the client (as is true with most styles of massage). If you like hard pressure, the therapist can use hard pressure and still give a good relaxing massage. If you like light pressure, this can be done as well.

Deep Tissue — This is where specific areas, usually problem areas are worked for a fairly long period of time. Usually this is done to correct problems like muscle pulls or other injuries.

Neuromuscular — This style of Deep Tissue massage is specifically designed to work out muscular and nerve problems.

Shiatsu — This is pressure point massage where various amounts of pressure is applied using the fingertips only. There are many points on the body that affect various functions that can benefit from this type of massage.

Hot Stone — This is where smooth stones are heated and then rubbed on the body after it has had oil or some lubricant applied. The heat from the stones permeates the muscles, making them relax and expand. If you like heat, this is very relaxing.

Chair Massage — This usually includes pressure and some rubbing. This type of massage is something you would normally see in an airport or office. The client sits in a massage chair and remains clothed, and no lubricant is used. The back and arms are usually rubbed and pressed to bring temporary relief of pain or fatigue. Deep Tissue massage can not be done during a chair massage session, and massage on skin is limited to light pressure. A chair massage session usually lasts from five to 15 minutes.

Myofascial — This type of massage is more energy work than physical rubbing. The therapist will listen to what you say your problems are, and then place her hands in various positions on the body to make a change in the energies. In most cases, this needs to be skin on skin contact as the energies of the therapist come into play. This method is good at finding problems in the body that could have been caused by changes in it from many years previously, like injuries or surgeries.

Massage does help the body heal and return to its natural well-being. Basically, as a therapist starts working an area, it becomes softer, more pliable, and less painful. One thing to keep in mind is that you may go to a therapist with a specific problem, and they will probably work more than that area. For example, you might come in with a sore back, and the therapist would work your entire body, or the entire back side. Or you might come in with pulled muscles in your legs, and the therapist will also work your back. To work a small area of the body will help, up to a certain point, but because all the muscles connect with one another, this is why more than one area is worked in that session. A low back problem can cause shoulder pain or leg pain because when we have problems, we change what we are doing or how we are walking to compensate for that problem.

Before starting a massage session on a client that they have never worked on before, a therapist will either ask them to fill out a medical questionnaire or ask health-related questions themselves. This may sound invasive, but it is for your protection as well as the therapist. When reviewing the information, a therapist will look for several things.

- ༀ The first thing they look for is if you are currently suffering from some contagious illness, like a cold or flu. In this case, the therapist cannot work on you in order to avoid spreading the illness and passing it on to someone else.
- ༀ The next thing they look for is a condition that would be worsened or cause you further problems if you received a massage. There are specific illnesses or injuries that would become worse if a therapist worked on you. These are called contraindications. Conditions that will be worse are cancers, any swelling (after swelling goes down it is OK), varicose veins, and any disease that is contagious. In the case of injuries, massage usually cannot be applied to the injured area while the injury is recent or acute. After a few days and you have had a chance to rest the injured area, massage would be helpful in bringing it back to full health.
- ༀ The final thing to look for is if you have any conditions, injuries, or are taking any medications that would affect the way

the therapist works on you. If you had an injury, the therapist would not want to do deep tissue work in the area of the injury. If you are taking certain drugs that might make you bruise easily, the therapist would not want to use heavy pressure.

The bottom line is that a licensed massage therapist is concerned about the well-being and comfort of her clients. They will not do anything willingly to hurt them, and will do everything they can to improve their condition while promoting relaxation and good health. A good massage is a wonderful experience. As stated before, massage has many benefits on the systems of the body, such as better feeling muscles, better blood flow, a cleansing of the system, and relaxation.

THE BENEFICIAL EFFECTS OF MASSAGE

- ଔ Massage relaxes muscle spasm and relieves tension and stress.
- ଔ Massage improves muscle tone.
- ଔ Massage lessens pain and facilitates movement and flexibility.
- ଔ Massage has a calming effect on the nervous system.
- ଔ Massage calms tightened muscles, enhancing one's sleep and freedom of movement.
- ଔ Massage helps lessen inflammation and swelling in joints, and in turn alleviates pain.
- ଔ Massage promotes well being, both physically, mentally and spiritually. You will feel better overall.
- ଔ Massage dilates the blood vessels, improving the circulation and relieving congestion throughout the body, therefore promoting healing and total wellness.
- ଔ Massage increases blood supply and nutrition to muscles.
- ଔ Massage encourages the retention of nitrogen, phosphorus, and sulfur necessary for tissue repair and new growth.
- ଔ Massage acts as a "mechanical cleanser" stimulating lymph circulation and helping with the elimination of wastes, toxic debris, and medications.

CONDITIONS THAT CAN IMPROVE WITH MASSAGE
- ⚬ improved blood flow
- ⚬ better muscle tone
- ⚬ better skin tone
- ⚬ more flexibility with muscles
- ⚬ less stress built up in your body, which in turn slows down illness and other conditions
- ⚬ peace of mind
- ⚬ longevity and overall good health
- ⚬ over all general health and well-being

WHERE DO I FIND A THERAPIST ?
Once you decide that you would like to try massage, whether to help with specific problems you are having or just to have a nice experience and de-stress, you need to choose a therapist. There are a number of places to look, and some as easy as the local Yellow Pages.

- ⚬ Look in the local Yellow Pages under Massage.
- ⚬ Ask your doctor or chiropractor to recommend someone.
- ⚬ Ask friends or coworkers if they know and recommend someone.
- ⚬ Ask other holistic / healing practitioners who they use or recommend
- ⚬ Look on the Internet: By typing "massage" and your town on a search engine, you can get a list of those therapists in your area.
- ⚬ Call the Chamber of Commerce in your area.
- ⚬ Call your state massage therapy association.
- ⚬ Ask people at your local health food or holistic stores.

HOW TO DECIDE WHO TO CONTACT
Ask yourself these questions:
- ⚬ Do you prefer a male therapist or a female therapist?
- ⚬ Do you prefer to go to a therapist's office, or would you prefer them to come to the privacy of your own home?

ભ Many therapists do "outcalls / housecalls" which is where they will come out to your home or motel room if you are out of town.

ભ You get the same quality work whether you go to them, or they come to you.

ભ Call the massage schools in your area. They might recommend some of their former students. Also, most schools have periods where they allow people to come in to get massage from a student. This is not as good as from a practiced, licensed therapist, but it usually costs less.

WHAT QUESTIONS DO I ASK THE MASSAGE THERAPIST WHEN I CALL?

ભ What kind of massage techniques / styles do they use.

ભ How long have they been doing massage.

ભ Ask how much they charge and for how long.

ભ How far in advance do you have to schedule an appointment with them.

ભ Do they have any referrals you can call to see how others like their work.

Tell them about any specific problems you have and why you are seeking their services; allow them to recommend different methods or techniques. If you are looking for a therapist, and have doubts because of some health problem or condition you have, call and ask questions. The key is that you want to find someone with whom you are comfortable. Once you do that, schedule a session, relax, and enjoy!

Recommended readings for additional information:
The Book of Massage by Lucinda Lidell
The New Sensual Massage by Gordon Inkeles

Raindrop Therapy and La Stone Therapy

The Raindrop Therapy is a powerful, non-invasive healing treatment originating from the research of D. Gary Young. Nine essential oils are dispensed one at a time from a height of six inches above the spine. Valor, one of these oils, gives a feeling of strength, courage and protection to the client. Each oil is massaged along the vertebrae and has its own unique fragrant influence. Hot compresses complete the treatment, activating the oils to reduce pain and inflammation and restore balance. The oils continue to work in the body for five to seven days following the treatment. Every organ, muscle and bone are stimulated at a cellular level, resulting in a release of toxins and a boost to the immune system. The heady, fragrant aroma of the oils lingers in the air well after the treatment is over. That's because five of these oils are well-known herbs. The Raindrop Treatment is wonderfully relaxing and balancing.

LASTONE THERAPY

LaStone Therapy, The Original Hot Stone Massage, was created by Mary Nelson Hannigan of Tucson, Arizona. The treatment combines the grounding power of the earth and the therapeutic benefits of massage to create a wonderful, healing therapy. Since the beginning of time, Shamans and Spiritual Healers have used stones in their healing ceremonies. The heated basalt stones represent the Yang, or male energy, and help to calm the mind and emotions. Marble stones are cool by nature and represent the Yin, or female energy, which help heighten one's awareness.

An assessment of the client's needs determines their personalized therapy. By alternating the use of hot and cool stones, circulation and detoxification are both increased, facilitating the healing procesS. With the client lying in the supine position, a short blessing or prayer is followed by a spinal layout using hot and/or cool stones. Proper chakra stone placement is followed by an application of warm oil to the body. and the massage begins. The velvety-smooth wet stones gliding over the oiled skin creates a wonderful, soothing feeling. The heat from the stones is quickly absorbed by the body and deeply relaxes the muscles. The cool stones are perfect for relieving pain and inflammation. Working with the client's breath, the chakras stones are removed, and the client turns to begin the final phase of the treatment.

Chinese fluorite is commonly used in the final closing technique to balance the fluid in the spine and create a very deep state of relaxation.

Smudging with sage and feather fan and/or the use of sound created by a Tibetan bowl, rain stick, or rubbing stones together helps the client bring their awareness back into the room and their body. It is not unusual for the client to experience an altered state of mind or have visions in their dream state during this deeply relaxing treatment.

The full effects of LaStone Therapy are felt three to five days after the treatment. Healing at all levels occurs physically, mentally, emotionally, and spiritually.

Chapter Nine

Dolphins and Their Wonderful Healing Abilities

Who are the Dolphins, really? Dolphins are master healers and keepers of the light upon Planet Earth. They are highly evolved beings who live in the Oneness. Their role is similar to that of the angelic kingdom. They are here to watch over us, to help and support us, and to guide us on our path to radiant wholeness. Their love for humanity is profound.

Like the angels, the dolphins' influence transcends time, space, and physicality. It is not necessary to be in their physical presence to be healed by them and to receive their gifts. Now, more than ever before, humanity as a whole is ready and willing to receive the profound gifts the dolphins have to share.

For me, the dolphins are my friends, my family, my healers, and my teachers. They make me laugh. They make me cry. They love me no matter what. The dolphins provided the unconditional love and safety I needed to do my healing, so that my profound love for myself...for this planet...for humanity...for all of life...could rise to the surface and be expressed without fear. The dolphins have helped me to love, accept and fully embrace my humanity. I am a better person, because of the dolphins.

Here is my personal story of my healing with dolphins while swimming in Hawaii:

During the summer of 1996, I decided to go on a spiritual vacation to Hawaii and swim with dolphins. I had heard dolphins are healing animals, and I was willing to try anything to get well. I read all I could get my hands on about dolphins and their healing abilities. I could hardly wait because I just knew they would help me get well. I went with a girlfriend, and on our fourth day, we got to swim with them — out in the wild blue ocean!!

When we got out of the boat and into the water, everyone headed for shore, except me. I could not see what they were following, and just then I saw something out of the corner of my eye. So I headed that way, which was towards the open ocean !! **Seven dolphins** *soon surrounded me, and they were guiding me out to the middle of the Pacific Ocean! I couldn't touch them because they were just out of my range, but they were so breathtaking, I didn't care. I couldn't believe I had seven dolphins all to myself. Then, all of a sudden, they disappeared into the bottom of the ocean, and I stopped swimming. I looked up and couldn't see anything or anyone. I finally saw a small white dot in the far distance, and I assumed that was the boat.*

Oh well, I thought. Guess I'll just have to swim back! At least I was a good swimmer! I started to snorkel back and all of a sudden the dolphins **reappeared** *and guided me back to the boat!! I took some pictures, but in my mind I was thinking no one would believe that I had seven dolphins of my own. Boy, I wish they would make an appearance, and as soon as I got my feet on the ladder and was safely back on the boat, they individually jumped over the bow of the boat, all seven of them!! The whole boatful of people began cheering!! After talking about my experience, I started to draw them in my notebook and to write my messages and feelings down. I felt blessed and healed. When we went to group discussion that evening, I talked a lot and everyone was tickled with my stories. I did manage to get a few photos while out there.*

I wrote this song after my encounter with the dolphins:

**SONG I HEARD IN MY SLEEP IN KONA, HAWAII -
DEDICATED FROM MY
ANGELS TO MY DOLPHIN SPIRIT GROUP**

ANGELS AMONG US
ANGELS SURROUND US

WE COME TO TEACH YOU,
GUIDE YOU, AND LOVE YOU

ANGELS AMONG US
ANGELS SURROUND US

WE'RE HERE TO SUPPORT YOU
AND SHOW YOU, THE WAY

ANGELS AMONG US
ANGELS SURROUND US

WE SHOW UP IN MANY
FORMS, SHAPES AND TONES

SO PLEASE LET US GUIDE
YOU,
LOVE YOU AND TEACH YOU
SO THAT YOU CAN GROW
TO LEVELS BEYOND.

Upon returning home from Hawaii, I proceeded to make dolphins my main focus in my designs and they became the number one selling item in my entire line.

DOLPHIN ENERGY HEALING SESSIONS

More and more people are feeling attracted to dolphins because of their innate sense that the dolphins can help them. Yet it is not possible, or practical, for everyone who loves dolphins to go to swim with them in the ocean. In a dolphin energy healing session, you receive the same energy, and often more, than you would if you were swimming with the dolphins physically.

In a session, you and your Divine Self co-create your experience with the energy and consciousness of the dolphins. Because the dolphins live in the Oneness, they serve as a bridge to All That Is.

You set the intention for what you would like to receive from the session, and your Dolphin Energy Practitioner holds the space for the healing and transformation to occur. The practitioner also serves as a vehicle for the dolphin love energy to flow through. The practitioner does not manipulate this energy in any way.

Healings can be given in person or remotely by telephone. It is always amazing how profound these remote healing sessions can be - there truly is no difference if the client is on the massage table or in another part of the world.

Here are a few things you can do to maximize your healing experience:

- ๛ Enter into the healing session with an open heart and mind. Release all expectations. Be open for your highest good to occur.
- ๛ Be clear in your intention to release any and all limiting thoughts, beliefs, and behaviors that no longer serve you; and be open and willing to receive the higher vibrational frequencies that do.
- ๛ Consider investing in a series of sessions. While each session is profound, the healing process is an unwinding of the old, and a bringing-to-the-surface of what is real and true. A series of sessions allows for the deepest release and the highest level of awakening to occur.

The dolphins live in a state of sheer exuberant joy of being alive, our inherently natural state of being, so yearned for by everybody yet so painfully inaccessible to most of humanity. Without exception, whether in the wild or in the brutal enslavement and debilitating conditions of marine parks, dolphins always bring people back to such a deep experience of their own joy, their own essence, to a place of love.

The dolphins, with all their cousins the Whales, are in the order of mammals called Cetacea, all highly developed beings with very large and complex brains. It has been clearly shown scientifically that the dolphins have a brain proportionately larger than humans and in some ways far more developed. They have clearly identifiable, highly evolved emotions such as joy, compassion, humor, and emotional self-control, and they live in large complex social groups that live in great harmony.

The dolphins have been reaching out to humanity since before recorded history. This wonderful being does nothing to harm us, rather it saves us from drowning in the oceans, helps near-shipwrecked boats navigate through dangerous waters and even helps us to return to our long lost natural state of real "humanity," of joy, compassion and love. Much of man has truly lost his Spirit, and one thing that the dolphins are doing is to reflect to us our long lost essence, to engage with us intelligently and lovingly.

DOLPHIN FACTS OVERVIEW

Here are some quick facts and general information about dolphins. See the Dolphin Species Index for information specific to particular kinds of dolphins. Dolphins are warm-blooded and use the blow hold at the top of their heads to breathe air like other land animals although they live in the sea. They close this blowhole when diving underwater to prevent water from entering their lungs.

Dolphins have teeth, a four-chambered heart (like humans), and even have a light covering of hair. Dolphins give birth to live babies and nurse them like many animal mothers do. Mature female dolphins will give birth every two to three years. Porpoises and dolphins are related, but they are not the same animal. Dolphins have a larger forehead and round teeth and porpoises are slimmer and have flat teeth. Dolphins and whales are from the same family. In fact, dolphins are called "toothed whales" and the largest dolphin is the Killer Whale (Orca), which can grow to 20 to 30 feet in length. Bottle nosed dolphins, which are the most common dolphins, grow eight to nine feet long at adulthood.

There are 32 species of oceanic dolphins and five species of river dolphins. Bottlenose dolphins can easily swim three to seven miles per hour and can go over 20 miles per hour if required. Dolphins are quite intelligent. Scientists currently disagree on the dolphin's exact intelligence level, but most agree it is along the same lines as a chimpanzee or a pig. However, the brain size of a bottle-nosed dolphin is similar to a human brain, so no one is exactly sure just how intelligent they may really be. Some experts say the intelligence order of mammals is 1) humans, 2) dolphins, 3) chimpanzee, 4) pig.

Dolphins can learn various actions to help them communicate with humans, if those actions are broken down into smaller steps. Training is similar to training other animals with a reward of food when done correctly. Dolphins communicate among themselves by using whistles and body actions, and have an extensive vocabulary in their language. They also use clicking sound pulses to help them navigate through the water. The sound pulses bounce off objects and let the dolphin know what is ahead and how large the object is.

The life span of a dolphin is 25 to 50 years. Dolphins have astute sound, keen vision, touch, and taste senses, although they cannot smell. A dolphin's diet consists of fish, crustaceans, and squid when available. Dolphins can be found in both the Pacific and Atlantic oceans and they prefer warm to tropical waters.

A few research centers in the world work in partnership with healthcare facilities and individual therapists from a variety of therapeutic disciplines. These programs can impact a wide population of children and adults with disabilities, improve their quality of life, and strengthen their human spirit. Autism, Down's syndrome, deaf and hard of hearing, cerebral palsy, vision impairment, spinal cord injuries, cancer, attention deficit disorder, and post-traumatic stress disorder are some of the disabilities and illnesses with which these dolphins work. These programs work with different therapies as well as new approaches, allowing them to match up people's specific needs with specialized therapists. They also offer more opportunities to conduct research.

It is an alternative therapy, which supports the work done in conventional therapies such as physical, occupational, or speech therapy. It is conducted by a professional therapist who utilizes the dolphin as both a stimulus to generate positive behaviors and as a reward for the child's efforts. Wonderful things may happen during the therapy;

however, dolphin-assisted therapy is not a "magical cure" for any disability, but rather a unique form of therapy, which aims for progress in specific therapy goals.

Participants swim with and/or interact with dolphins in goal-oriented activities designed to help participants improve their physical, cognitive and communication skills; these activities also help to increase their self-esteem, while decreasing their anxiety and depression levels. Educational and recreational activities are introduced during the dolphin-assisted therapy to increase motivation and to enhance the participant's abilities.

Through participation in the program, participants learn to feel more positive about themselves in an environment that promotes fun and play. They are able to forget about their stressful situations while learning new behaviors, actions, and learning strategies. The end goals of the program are to increase the participants' self-concept, to decrease their level of depression and anxiety, to help the participants' communicate more effectively with the people within their environment, and most of all, to have a fun time away from the stress of medical, physical, or emotional concerns. The dolphin interaction provides positive reinforcement for the child upon accomplishment of appropriate behaviors. It may include behaviors related to speech, language, fine or gross motor skill development, and rote or conceptual thinking.

Many of the interactions are paid for by the individual, their family, or friends. On occasion, the participants may be sponsored by "wish granting" organizations such as Make-A-Wish Foundation, Sunshine Foundation, Starlight Foundation, Children's Wish Foundation, The Dream Foundation, Dream Come True, Dream Factory, Easter Seal Society, Children's Hope and Dream Foundation, or any of the various foundations worldwide. A "wish" to swim or interact with dolphins offers a welcome respite from the stress of dealing with a serious illness as well as providing motivation to reach beyond current capabilities. Swimming and playing with dolphins is like a moment of magic to many.

It is a feeling of wonder and privilege, love and joy as you witness the mingling of dolphin and human spirits. It happens when you hear a child who has never spoken before say a dolphin's name or say "I love you."

DOLPHIN TRAVEL DESTINATIONS: AQUARIUMS WITH DOLPHINS

Planning a vacation in the near future? If so, you may want to stop and visit some of these amazing aquariums, many of which feature the opportunity to also swim with dolphins, and you don't have to have an illness or disability to participate. Go do it, you will love it, and it will change your life forever!! I promise!! Do you live too far away, but want to swim with them now? Try ordering my dolphin meditation CD and you can be swimming with them in the privacy of your own home. ENJOY!!

Clearwater Marine Aquarium
249 Windward Passage
Clearwater, Florida 33767-2244
Toll Free: (888) 239-9414
Voice:727-441-1790

Dolphin Encounters
P.O. Box N-7448
Nassau, Bahamas
Voice: 242-363-1003

The Dolphin Experience
Sanctuary Bay
P.O. Box F 43788
Freeport, Grand Bahama Island
The Bahamas
Voice: 242-373-3943

Dolphin Quest Bermuda
Fairmont Southampton Princess
P.O. Box HM1379
Hamilton HM FX
Bermuda
Voice:441-239-6957

Dolphin Quest Hawaii
The Big Island
Hilton Waikoloa Village
69-425 Waikoloa Beach Drive
Waikoloa, HI 96738
Voice: 808-886-2875

Dolphin Quest Moorea
InterContinental
Beachcomber Resort Moorea
PO Box 1021, Papetoai,
Moorea 98729
French Polynesia
Voice: 011-689-55-1948

Dolphin Quest Oahu
Kahala Mandarin Oriental Resort
5000 Kahala Avenue
Honolulu, HI 96816
Voice: 808-739-8918

Dolphin Research Center
P.O. Box 522875
Marathon Shore, FL 33052
Voice: 305-289-1121

Gulf World
15412 Front Beach Road
Panama City Beach, FL 32413
Voice: 850-234-5271

John G. Shedd Aquarium
1200 South Lake Shore Drive
Chicago, Illinois 60605
Voice: 312.939.2435

The Living Seas Pavillion-Epcot Center
2020 N. Avenue of the Stars
Lake Buena Vista, FL 32830
Voice: 407-560-5344

Miami Seaquarium
4400 Rickenbacker Causeway
Miami, FL 33149
Voice: 305-365-2535

Mystic Aquarium
55 Coogan Boulevard
Mystic, CT 06355
Voice: 860-572-5955

Sea Life Park Hawaii
41-150 Kalanianaole Highway
Makapuu Point
Waimanalo, HI 96795
Voice: 808-259-2533

Sea World San Diego
500 SeaWorld Drive
San Diego, CA 92109
Voice: 619-226-3900

Sea World of Florida
7007 Sea World Drive
Orlando, FL 32821
Voice: 407-363-2364

Sea World of Texas
10500 Sea World Drive
San Antonio, TX 78251
Voice: 210-523-3277

Six Flags Marine World
2001 Marine World Parkway
Vallejo, CA 94589
Voice: 707-643-6722

Theater of the Sea
84721 Overseas Highway
Islamorada, FL 33036
Voice: 305-664-8189

Vancouver Aquarium Marine
Science Center
P.O. Box 3232
Vancouver, BC V6B3X8
Canada
Voice: 604-659-3583

Dolphin Swim Facilities and Programs

Dolphin Discover
Isla Mujeres, Mexico
Voice: 52-98-830779,830780

Dolphin Encounters
Blue Lagoon Island Salt Cay
Nassau, Bahamas
Voice: 242-363-1003
FAX: 242-327-5059

Dolphins Plus
31 Corrine Place
Key Largo, Florida 33037
Voice: 305-451-1993

Dolphin Reef Eliat
Southern Beach
P.O.Box 104
Eilat 88100, Israel
Voice: 972-7-371846,373417
FAX: 972-7-375921

Dolphin Research Center
Mile Marker 59, Highway US 1
Grassy Key, Florida 33050
Voice: 305-289-1121

Dolphin Retreats
14640 SW 87 Court
Miami, Florida 33176
Voice/FAX: 305-235-0297

Living From the Heart
P.O. Box 987
Morrison, Colorado 80465
Voice: 800-627-4753
Voice: 303- 697-4084

Theatre of the Sea
Mile Marker 84, Highway US 1
Islamorada, Florida 33036
Voice: 305-664-2431

*Dolphin-Guided Open Swim
Programs*

Anthony's Key Resort
Sandy Bay, Roatan
Honduras, Central America
Voice: 800-227-3483
FAX: 011-504-445-1329

UNEXSO
P.O. Box 42433
Freeport, Grand Bahama
Island, The Bahamas
Voice: 242 373-1244
FAX: 242 373-8956

Wild Dolphin Dive Excursions

Dancing Dolphin Institute
P.O. Box 959
Kihei, Maui, Hawaii 96753
Reservations: 808-879-7044

The Dolphin Circle
P O Box 1426
Lake Stevens, WA 98258
Voice: 206-334-0272
FAX: 206-397-0775

Dolphin Discover Centre
P.O. Box 1178
Bunbury, Western Australia
6231
Voice: 011 61 97 91 3088
FAX: 011 61 97 913420

Dolphinswim with Rebecca
Fitzgerald
P.O. Box 8653
Santa Fe, New Mexico 87504
FAX: 505-466-0579

Dolphin Synergy
Voice: 505-986-1215
Fax: 505-986-1207

Dolphin Watch
Capt. Ron Canning
Key West, FL
Voice: 305 294 6306

Dolphin Trips
620 N. Coppell Rd. Suite 3804
Coppell, TX 75019
Voice: 972-745-2782
crudy@dolphintrip.com

Dream Team Wild Dolphin
Adventures
P.O. Box 12174
Lake Park, FL 33403-2174
(888) 277-8181 Toll Free
Voice: 561-848-5375
FAX: 561-840 7946

Capt. Vicki Impallomeni
1737 Laird St.
Key West, FL 33040
Voice: 305-294-9731

WildQuest
Voice: 800-326-1618
FAX: 305-294-0365

CHAPTER Ten

The Many Uses of Aromatherapy Oils and Herbs

Essential oils are the building blocks of aromatherapy. The oils are produced from plant materials by distillation or other processes. Parts used include flowers, roots, leaves, berries, seeds, or fruits. The quality of the oil is determined by purity, type of distillation or plant variety. It is always best to use the purest oils. Oils can be used several different ways, such as massage, bath, inhalation, steam vapor inhalation, chest rub, aromatic diffuser, spray mist/air refresher, skin care, and hair care. Each different use is listed next to the various aromatherapy oil.

EXPLANATION OF TECHNIQUES:

Massage: Add 10-12 drops of chosen essential oil to 1 ounce of massage oil. I would suggest using one of the following oils to mix your essential oil with: sweet almond, apricot, almond, apricot, avocado, grape seed, hazelnut, olive, or canola.

Baths: Use only 3-8 drops and pour into running water. If it is recommended you dilute the oil first, then add 1 tablespoon of vegetable oil to the essential oil before adding to bath water.

Steam Inhalation: Use 5-12 drops of essential oil in 2-4 cups of water. Bring water to a boil, let cool for 1 minute; then cover head with a towel, close your eyes and inhale the steam vapors for a few minutes.

Or use a facial steam machine. Try a few drops on a tissue or handkerchief and simply inhale the aromatic fragrance. Also, try putting it on your pillow at night

Chest rub: Use formula for massage oil and rub into chest and back

Diffusers: use a commercial machine to effectively vaporize and disperse essential oils into the air. Great way to refresh the air, kill airborne bacteria and promote physical and emotional health.

Spray Mist/Air Refresher: Add 10-20 drops of favorite essential oil to a spray bottle of purified water and shake before each use.

Skin Care: You can add essential oils to your facial cleanser, toners, and lotions by mixing 10-15 drops to 1-ounce liquid.

You can also add these essential oils to facial steams and saunas:

NORMAL SKIN: geranium, lavender, Neroli, and rose.

DRY SKIN: chamomile, Neroli, rose, sandalwood

OILY SKIN: bergamot, cedarwood, cypress, geranium, lavender, lemon

SENSITIVE SKIN: chamomile, jasmine, Neroli, rose

AGED SKIN/WRINKLES: frankincense, jasmine, Neroli, patchouli, rose

CHAPPED SKIN: benzoin, chamomile, geranium, rose sandalwood

Hair Care:

DRY/DAMAGED HAIR: geranium, sandalwood and ylang ylang: Mix 10-15 drops per 1 oz of jojoba oil and massage into scalp and hair, can leave in hair or apply heat for 30 minutes and then shampoo.

OILY HAIR: rosemary, cedarwood, lavender, clary sage Mix 5-10 drops into 16 oz warm water and use as a final rinse after shampooing

HAIR GROWTH: cedarwood, clary sage, rosemary and ylang ylang

DANDRUFF: cedarwood, patchouli, rosemary and tea tree

ESSENTIAL OILS AND THEIR QUALITIES AND USES:

BASIL   bronchitis, headaches, migraines, head colds, digestive aid, tired and sore muscles, mouth ulcers, and
gum infections. Also eases mental fatigue, stimulates brain functions, clears the mind, and lifts depression.

Uses: bath, massage, diffuser, spray mist, mouthwash, hot/
cold compress.

Do not use if pregnant.

BERGAMOT   depression, stress, tension, appetite regulator, fear,
pms, menstrual regulator, acne, cold sores, immune
booster. Also use for peace, happiness, confidence,
courage, and restful sleep

Uses: bath, massage, diffuser, cold compresses

BLACK PEPPER digestive tract, muscle pain, stiff joints, kidneys.

Uses: massage, food additive

CEDARWOOD   nervous tension, anxiety, stimulates hair growth, antiseptic, tonic for kidneys, nervous and respiratory
systems. Anti-fungal, vaginal infections, bronchitis,
cystitis, regenerative, insect repellent. Also use for
spirituality and self-control.

Uses: bath, massage, chest rub, hot compress, inhalation,
sauna, diffuser, skin, and hair care.

Do not use during pregnancy.

CHAMOMILE   pain-relief, fevers, earaches, menstrual problems,
teething pain, sedative insomnia, rheumatism,
sprains, and nervousness. Lowers blood pressure
and eases congestion of liver and spleen. Aids in
healing of burns and wounds. Also promotes an
inner peace when one is feeling overwhelmed and
needs a caring touch.

Uses: bath, massage, diffuser, spray mist, cold compresses,
mouthwash, skin, and hair care.

CINNAMON   infections, coughs, colds, flue, rheumatism, urinary
                     tract infections, stomach irritation, tooth decay,
                     arthritis, aches and pains, physical energy, psychic
                     awareness and prosperity.

Uses: capsules, herbal tea, toothpaste, and tinctures. Nev-
                     er ingest Cinnamon Oil as it could cause nausea,
                     vomiting and possibly even kidney damage.

CLARY SAGE   muscular fatigue, menstrual problems, PMS, asth-
                     ma, exhaustion, insomnia, menopausal problems
                     and cramps, calming, stress, and depression. Relax-
                     es muscles and stimulates the scalp to promote hair
                     growth. Also good for deep sleep and vivid
                     dreams.

Uses: bath, massage, diffuser, spray mist, skin, hot
                     compress, and hair care.

Do not use if pregnant.

CLOVES   toothache, muscle pain, tired limbs, colds, flu,
                     strep throat, diarrhea, intestinal worms,
                     digestive problems, vomiting, bronchitis,
                     memory, protection, and courage.

Uses: mouthwash, essential oils, capsules, in-
                     fusion, diffuser, and toothache pain-relief
                     preparations.

CORIANDER   rheumatism, pain, digestion, and stimulates appe-
                     tite.

Uses: bath, massage

Do not use if pregnant.

CYPRESS   circulation, menopausal and menstrual problems,
                     coughs, asthma, fluid retention, cellulite, hemor-
                     rhoids, rheumatism, tensions, and nervousness. Also
                     eases the anxiety and stress, which accompany life's
                     changes and transitions.

Uses: bath, massage, sauna, diffuser, spray mist.

EUCALYPTUS Bronchitis, colds, flu, fever, sinusitis, muscular aches, asthma, burns, and insect bites. Purifies room of negative energy and viruses. Use during and after being sick in the house to clear out germs and infections and keep from spreading. Also speeds physical and emotional healing processes, and alleviates grief and sorrow.

Uses: bath, massage, sauna, steam inhalation, chest rub, mouthwash, hot/cold compresses, diffuser, spray mist.

FENNEL   abdominal pain, flatulence, coughs, sore throats, digestive problems, PMS, fluid retention, purification, longevity, and courage.

Uses: bath, massage, mouthwash

Do not use if pregnant or on babies or children.

FRANKINCENSE reduces stress and tension, skin disorders, respiratory infections, circulation, depression, mental fatigue and awakens higher consciousness. Also promotes peaceful sleep and pleasant dreams and alleviate nightmares. Ideal for meditation and spiritual practices, by enhancing one's connection to spirit.

Uses: bath, massage, diffuser, steam inhalation, skin care

GERANIUM   fertility, circulation, anti-depressant, menopause, regulates menstrual cycle, pms, bruising, antibacterial.

Uses: bath, massage, diffuser, skin care, cold compress

GINGER   antiseptic, colds, flu, muscle fatigue, aphrodisiac, arthritis, nervous exhaustion, seasickness, travel sickness, morning sickness, stimulant, expectorant. Promotes courage, confidence, assertiveness, and enhances memory.

Uses: Bath, massage, diffuser, hot/cold compresses, mouthwash, steam inhalation

GRAPEFRUIT   cellulite, muscle fatigue, acne, blood circulation, headaches, mental exhaustion, eases depression and moodiness, energizes nervous system, hangovers, fluid retention and detoxification.

Uses: bath, massage, diffuser, spray mist

JASMINE   depression, fertility, nervous tension, menstrual pain, childbirth, cramps, coughs, skin care, dry skin, chest pains, and blockages, aphrodisiac, and sleep. Use for love, peace, spirituality and psychic abilities. Promotes creativity, imagination, fantasy and dreams.

Uses: bath, massage, skin care, diffuser.

JUNIPER   fluid retention, ulcers, arthritis, gout, eczema, cystitis, obesity, kidney and bladder disorders, mental exhaustion, acne, sciatica, and hay fever. Also wards off negativity and purifies your home. Promotes sense of well-being and inner strength

Uses: bath, massage, diffuser
Do not use if pregnant

LAVENDER   Headaches, cuts, burns, rheumatism, asthma, bronchitis, colds, flu, coughs, sore throats, insect bites, arthritis, anxiety, tension, panic attacks, menstrual pain, sleep. Helps reduce labor pain and calms the mother during childbirth. Also induces peace and dispels depression. Rub some on your pillows at night for a restful nights sleep. Also brings clarity, peace of mind, and emotional balance. Known as "the angel of healing and purification."

Uses: bath, massage, steam inhalation, chest rub, hot / cold compresses, sauna, diffuser, spray mist, skin, and hair care.

LEMON   stimulates immune system, warts, depression, confusion, bleeding gums, acne, digestion, diuretic, cellulite, and skin care. Promotes mental clarity and decisiveness.

Uses: bath (dilute), massage, steam inhalation, hot compress, chest rub, diffuser, mouthwash

LEMONGRASS infections, digestion, headaches, deodorant.
Uses: bath, massage, diffuser

MARIGOLD   dry skin, rashes, varicose veins, and chronic ulcers.
Uses: bath, massage, hot compress

MARJORAM   respiratory problems, colds, bronchitis, asthma, insomnia, blood pressure, heart problems, hysteria, nervous tension, irritability, worry, grief, rheumatism, arthritis, insomnia, pms.
Uses: bath, massage, steam inhalation, chest rub, diffuser
Do not use if pregnant.

MYRRH   mouth ulcers, digestion, eczema, acne, bronchitis, colds, catarrh, sore throats, stomach and promotes healing of cuts and wounds.
Uses: bath, massage, chest rub, steam inhalation diffuser, spray mist, skin care, mouthwash.
Do not use if pregnant.

MYRTLE   astringent, acne, bronchitis, hemorrhoids, infections.
Uses: bath, massage, diffuser, steam inhalation,

NEROLI   nervousness, calming, insomnia, pms, depression, tension, stretch marks, scar tissue, gums anti-spasmodic. Eases fear, depression, grief, shock, and hysteria. Brings inspiration, enhances creativity, and assist one in embracing and transforming negative emotions.
Uses: bath, massage, diffuser, spray mist, skin care, hair care, cold compresses

NUTMEG   circulation, bad breath, rheumatism, pain, heart problems.

Uses: massage, hot compresses, mouthwash, steam inhalation, diffuser

ORANGE   constipation, chronic diarrhea, stomach, mild sedative, obsessions, fear. Promotes mental clarity, emotional balance and assists one in resolving and releasing deep emotional issues.

Uses: bath, massage, diffuser, spray mist, mouthwash

PATCHOULI   acne, dandruff, eczema, skin problems, lethargy, confusion, depression, sedative, anxiety, stress, constipation, dandruff, insect repellent, fluid retention, substance addictions, and physical energy. Promotes individuality, centeredness, and stability.

Uses: bath, massage, diffuser, skin care, hair care, mouthwash

PEPPERMINT   headaches, nausea, colic, diarrhea, indigestion, vomiting, stomach pain, colds, fever, flu, fatigue, mouthwash, travel and motion sickness, and sinus congestion. Aids concentration, discernment, decisiveness, and sparks the inner child within; inspiring a sense of enthusiasm and excitement.

Uses: bath (dilute) massage, diffuser, spray mist, steam inhalation, mouthwash

Do not use if pregnant.

PINE   chest infections, colds, sore throats, bronchitis, gout, circulation, lungs, kidney and bladder problems, digestive stimulant, rheumatic pains.

Uses: diffuser, steam inhalation, chest rub (dilute) sauna, bath, spray mist

ROSE   fertility, female reproductive problems, depression, anorexia, tension, postnatal depression, sadness, grief, constipation, anxiety, headaches, and skin care. Also use for love, peace, sex, beauty and confidence builder. Helps ease envy, jealousy, resentment, and anger. Promotes creativity, appreciation of beauty and harmony and inspires one's heart.

Uses: bath, massage, skin care, diffuser, spray mist, steam inhalation, hair care

ROSEMARY muscular pain, heart, rheumatism, arthritis, sciatica, constipation, coughs, colds, bronchitis, memory enhancement, hangovers, over-indulgence, exhaustion, overworking muscles, acne, skin care, hair growth, and headaches. Promotes self-confidence, courage, mental clarity, and concentration.

Uses: massage, bath (dilute), chest rub, cold compresses, diffuser, spray mist, steam inhalation, skin, and hair care.

Do not use if pregnant, have epilepsy or high blood pressure.

SANDALWOOD bronchitis, coughs, sore throats, laryngitis, dry skin, cystitis, fluid retention, urinary infections, digestion, and depression. Promotes deep peaceful meditation and deepens one's connection to spirit.

Uses: bath, massage, steam inhalation, chest rub, skin care, sauna, diffuser.

TEA TREE OIL rashes, bronchitis, sore throats, colds, flu, asthma, bronchitis, Candida albicans, athletes foot, dandruff, influenza, acne, fatigue, insect bites, warts, nail fungus, burns, tooth and gum infections, cold sores, ringworm, head lice, and all viral infections. Also known as "the miracle oil." A must for any first aid kit.

Uses: bath, massage, steam inhalation, chest rub, diffuser, mouthwash.

THYME   congestion, colds, flu, muscular pain, arthritis, poor
                       circulation, gout, acne, warts, and all infections.
                       Also stimulates conscious mind.
Uses: chest rub, mouthwash, massage
Do not use if pregnant

VETIVER   rheumatism, menstrual problems, stress, tension,
                       worry, fear, insomnia, muscle relaxant, overindul-
                       gence, and protection. Promotes a sense of security
                       and stability. Also aids in development of patience
                       and stillness.
Uses: massage, bath, diffuser

YLANG YLANG nervousness, physical exhaustion, high blood pres-
                       sure, depression, stress, headaches, nausea, irrita-
                       bility, anxiety, pms, and hair growth. Also use for
                       peace, love and an aphrodisiac. Inspires creativity
                       and one's appreciation of beauty. Assist in overcom-
                       ing sexual difficulties.
Uses: bath, massage, diffuser, skin, and hair care.

HERBS AND VITAMINS AND THEIR BASIC USES

Alfalfa

Alfalfa is a member of the legume family. Alfalfa neutralizes acids and poisons, has a natural ability to stimulate and the feed the
pituitary gland, and it is a natural deodorizer. It also has the ability to
absorb and carry intestinal waste out of the body. Ancient Indian Ay-
urvedic physicians used Alfalfa to treat ulcers, arthritis pains and fluid
retention. Early Americans used Alfalfa to treat arthritis, boils, cancer, scurvy, and urinary and bowel problems. Pioneer women used it
to aid menstruation. Alfalfa has also been used traditionally for treating infections resulting from surgical incisions bed sores and inner ear
problems.

Aloe Vera

It has been used since ancient times, since it is known as a plant that heals. Aloe vera has properties for promoting new cell growth, stopping pain, and reducing the chance of infection and scarring. It is recommended in treating certain types of burns, like 3rd degree X-ray burn, radiation burns, and sunburns. In juice form, it will boost the immune system and increase digestion and absorption.

Vitamin B-Complex

Many different vitamin B compounds are grouped under the name B-complex. These vitamins are easily lost in refining and cooking; they can also be washed from the body by coffee, tea, alcohol, and heavy perspiration. Physically stressful conditions can also deplete the body of B vitamins. B vitamins are particularly important for the nervous system and are also vital for good digestive function and enzyme reactions that control energy, circulation, hormones, and overall health.

Bayberry

Bayberry inhibits bacteria and is useful in fighting infections, healing cuts, bruises, and insect bites. It is a stimulant, which helps to invigorate and strengthen the body and creates a resistance to disease. Contemporary herbalists recommend using the herb externally for varicose veins and internally for diarrhea, dysentery, colds, flu, bleeding gums, and sore throat.

Bee Pollen

Bee pollen, a true gift from Mother Nature, contains many essential nutrients. It is an excellent nutritional supplement for enhancing immunity and, with its strong nutritional profile, for providing energy. Bee pollen is often used during allergy season, and it also relieves other respiratory problems such as bronchitis, sinusitis, and colds. It contains up to 35 percent complete protein, 22 amino acids, a rich storehouse of B vitamins, 27 mineral salts, trace elements, and several enzymes. Greeks called it the "nectar of the gods."

Black Cohosh

Black Cohosh has been valued by many societies for its nutritional support of the female reproductive system and its abilities to balance hormone levels and hot flashes. Many women have found that black cohosh provides nutritional support during menopause. Black cohosh works directly on and calms the nervous system, as it relieves spasms and menstrual cramps. **It is effectively used for epilepsy and spinal meningitis.**

Black Walnut

Black walnut is a rich source of the trace mineral chromium and is also high in iodine. The ancient Greeks used the hulls to support the intestinal system and to treat skin infections. Taken internally, Black Walnut helps relieves constipation, and is also useful against fungal & parasitic infections. It may also help eliminate warts, which are troublesome growths caused by viruses. Rubbed on the skin, Black Walnut extract is reputed to be beneficial for eczema, herpes, psoriasis, and skin parasites. External applications have been known to kill ringworm. The Chinese use this herb to kill tapeworms with extremely good success.

Blessed Thistle

Blessed thistle helps improve digestion and aids in promoting proper liver function. It is useful with cramps, painful menstruation, headaches associated with female problems and as a hormone balancer. In Europe, the monks grew blessed thistle as a cure for smallpox. Blessed Thistle tea is used by contemporary herbalists for the treatment of a variety of liver problems, such as jaundice and hepatitis. Because painful menstruation can involve the liver, Blessed Thistle is a common component of herbal formulas used to relieve menstrual symptoms. Containing B-complex, calcium, iron, manganese, cincin and essential oils, Blessed Thistle can be used to increase the appetite and alleviate inflammation caused by poor digestion. Blessed Thistle also improves circulation and purifies the blood increasing oxygen to the brain to stimulate memory.

Burdock

Burdock is an excellent blood purifier and cleanser. It can reduce swelling around the joints by promoting kidney function, thus increasing the flow of urine. It is an herb used during pregnancy, as it helps balance all the systems and prevents water retention and jaundice in the baby. The Chinese have used it for coughs, colds, sore throats, tonsillitis, measles, sores, and abscesses.

Capsicum or Cayenne

It promotes perspiration, and increases thermo genesis (speed of fat metabolism) for weight loss. It is excellent in warding off diseases and equalizing blood circulation, which works to prevent strokes and heart attacks. Sprinkled in socks or shoes, it will prevent frostbite and aid in circulation. (No more cold feet !)

Cascara Sagrada

As a nutritional support for proper waste elimination, this bark has been used by cultures around the world. Cascara sagrada acts as an herbal laxative, which is an excellent choice for chronic constipation, cleanses, and restores a healthy colon. It also helpful in treatment of hemorrhoids and gallstones.

Catnip

Catnip was used by the American Indians for its sedative effect on the nervous system as well as treating colic in infants. It relieves pain, prevents spasms, and calms the nerves. It has been documented as normalizing blood pressure. Catnip works quickly to overcome epilepsy convulsions in children and control restlessness and colic by helping the body to rest. Catnip enemas cleanse the colon, relieve gas from the bowels, reduce spasms and can reduce fevers quickly.

Chamomile

Chamomile may be best known as a popular late-night herbal tea, as it soothes the nerves and promotes more restful sleep. It also aids in digestive and bowel problems. This herb is beneficial during pregnancy as it relaxes you for a sound sleep and helps with digestive and bowel problems. Catnip has soothing and relaxing effects on the digestive system, relieving diarrhea, flatulence, indigestion, upset stomach and headaches. Catnip contains antispasmodic properties that are ideal for treating abdominal and menstrual cramping, as well as chronic coughing. Excellent in reducing fevers, Catnip is also good for alleviating sleeplessness and insomnia. Catnip's antibiotic and astringent properties are also beneficial for treating colds and bronchial infections. This herb also has many topical application - as a bath herb for stress, colic and teething; as a compress or poultice for pain, sprains, bruises and insect bites; as a poultice for toothache; and as a hair rinse for scalp irritations. Other uses include Catnip as a liniment for arthritis & rheumatism; as an eyewash for inflammation, allergies and bloodshot eyes; as an enema to cleanse the colon; and as a salve for hemorrhoids.

Chaparral

In Mexico, it has been used for centuries as an anti-cancer remedy. Many universities has tested it and found it an aid in dissolving tumors and in fighting cancer. It also tones the system. It rebuilds tissue and is an effective healer for the urethra tract, blood, liver, and lymphatic systems.

Chickweed

Chickweed was used by the North American Chippewa and Iroquois Indians as an eyewash and wound poultice, applied directly to boils, burns and sores. It relieves sore throats, lowers fevers, and treats stomach and duodenal ulcers. It is good for sore eyes and allergies and has been used to break down cellulite.

Chlorophyll

Chlorophyll is the green pigment in plants that harnesses the sun's energy in photosynthesis. Liquid Chlorophyll helps improve immune response, deodorize the body, and cleanses the blood of impurities. Is also an anemia blood builder and supports the liver's function in detoxification. In certain religious groups, chlorophyll has been used in place of blood transfusions before, during, and after operations.

Cinnamon

Cinnamon works to help calm down the stomach, reduce milk flow in pregnant women and stop excessive menstrual flow. It is also useful for discomfort of chest pains, back and neck pains, and pain in menopause.

Comfrey

Comfrey has been used as a healing herb since 400 BC. It was known to have the power to encourage body tissue repair. The Greeks used it to stop heavy bleeding and treat bronchial problems. The general rule in herbology is "if anything is broken, use comfrey," as it is an excellent healer. Pouring a fluid extract of comfrey into a wound often closes the wound and helps avoid the need for stitches. Comfrey is one of the greatest herbs God has ever given man, and the FDA wants to remove it from the market.

Colloidal Minerals

Colloidal minerals help meet your body's need for active enzyme systems, chemical balance, maintenance, and repair of all body systems and minerals to act with the body's many metabolic regulators.

Colloidal Silver

Research indicates that colloidal silver is an effective antimicrobial, deactivating the enzymes responsible for the metabolism and multiplication of bacteria, fungi, and viruses. Colloidal silver has become a popular alternative to other natural antimicrobial products on the market.

Corn Silk

Corn silk has been used for centuries for kidney problems, inflamed bladders, and the prostrate gland. Physicians have used it as a diuretic, and is excellent for the elderly with urinary troubles or for the very young with bedwetting problems. Corn silk is very popular in Chinese herbology.

Damiana

Damiana was used by the Maya Indians for lung disorders, dizziness, vertigo and as a general body cleanser. Damiana supports glandular health and is specifically sought to support sexual health. The Aztecs used it as an aphrodisiac. It is one of the herbs of choice for helping with sexual impotency and infertility for both men and women. It helps women with menopause, hot flashes, and hormone balancing. It has been recommended for increasing sperm count in the male.

Dandelion

Herbalists consider this plant one of the most nutrient-rich in the plant kingdom, and it is a superior natural diuretic. The juice of the dandelion root is used in Europe to treat diabetes and liver diseases. The juice can also be used to treat warts, acne, blisters, and corns. The Chinese have used dandelion for breast cancer for over a thousand years and use the seeds as a strong antibiotic in cases of lung infections.

Dong Quai

Dong Quai is considered the queen of herbs by the Chinese and is China's most popular herb for women. Chinese physicians use the herb to enrich the blood, promote circulation, regulate menstruation, calm nerves, and soothe the intestines. Dong Quai may also be used to boost metabolism, reduce cholesterol, aid digestion, and relieve pain caused by arthritis. Other uses for Dong Quai are to increase the absorption of oxygen by the liver and purify the blood, therefore nourishing the brain, heart, and spleen.

Echinacea

Echinacea has been known as one of the best alternatives for detoxifying the blood. It cleanses the lymphatic system and supports the immune system. It is also used to treat strep and sore throats. Echinacea activates the body's defense system against all outside influences and viruses. This herb is beneficial and safe during pregnancy, as it is an immune system stimulant, which helps prevent infections. Echinacea is one of the best-selling herbs worldwide. This herbal immune booster is one of the most respected and widely used herbs thanks to the large amount of research that illustrates it's potential benefits. Research has demonstrated that Echinacea stimulates the production of white blood cells to fight infection. This is one herb no family should be without. There are no side effects to this herb.

Eucalyptus Oil

It is useful during the cold weather season. It contains strong antibacterial, antifungal, antiseptic, and antiviral compounds. It is most widely used as a steam inhalation for its antiseptic and stimulating effects in bronchitis, asthma, croup, flu, and pneumonia. It can also be rubbed directly on the chest or back to relieve congestion in the lungs.

Feverfew

Feverfew grows widely across Europe and North America and is an effective treatment for migraine headaches. Since the Middle Ages, this herb has been used to reduce fevers. Feverfew has been used, like aspirin, primarily as a pain buffer. Helping regulate normal body functions, Feverfew works with the body to help heal itself. Used to relieve severe headaches, migraines and reduce fevers by cooling the body, Feverfew also helps to ease a wide range of ailments. Reducing inflammation, Feverfew is used for relieving pain linked to arthritis and reducing painful menstruation.

Folic Acid

Folic acid is essential for human health, especially for the developing fetus. Deficiencies in folic acid have been linked to neural tube defects that affect the brain and spinal cord. Its potential to reduce the risk of neural tube defects is so important that the Food and Drug Administration now requires food manufacturers to fortify enriched grain products with folic acid.

Garlic

Garlic is a member of the family that includes onions, leeks, and shallots. An old Welsh saying goes, "Eat leeks in March and wild garlic in May, and all the year after physicians may play." This prized herb possesses antibiotic (natural penicillin), antiviral, antibacterial, and anti fungal properties. Garlic is effective in treating arthritis and may prevent breast cancer, heart disease, strokes, and some viral infections. It is an anti-tumor agent used as a preventive for many types of cancer and other degenerative diseases. It helps control disorders of the blood and is good for expelling parasites from the colon, when used internally or in enema form. It strengthens and nourishes the heart and has a positive effect on the stomach, spleen, and lungs. Garlic is one of many Super Foods that some consider to be one of the most potent healing herbs in the world.

Ginger

Ginger has been cultivated for thousands of years in China and India. It was written about in many ancient Chinese herbal texts and is an ingredient in as many as half of all Chinese herbal combinations. Ginger helps to settle the stomach and increase circulation, especially to the feet and hands. Many people use it to help prevent nausea, motion sickness and to support the female body during morning sickness.

Ginkgo

You know this supplement as Ginkgo Biloba, one of the five top-selling herbs in the US. A powerful free radical, ginkgo helps protect blood vessels and optimizes the amount of oxygen supplied to brain cells, which improves memory and concentration. It also helps increase blood flow to the nervous system, and aids in treatment of dementia and Alzheimer's disease.

Ginseng

It is believed to help balance the body and help the body adapt to stress. Ginseng is also famed for its ability to boost energy, fight fatigue and depression, and support the immune system. It also has a tonic effect on the pituitary gland and a stimulating effect on your adrenals. It has a history of improving the adrenal flow from your adrenals, which makes it effective at combating male impotence. In women, ginseng is known to produce testosterone, therefore it not recommended for use over long period of time.

Ginseng, Siberian

Siberian ginseng helps many nervous disorders and helps one when under mental or physical exhaustion. It improves sleep, appetite, and reflex action in those suffering from chronic anxiety. Siberian ginseng can be taken by both men and women over a long period of time.

Golden Seal

Early on, the pioneers followed the Indians' example in using this herb to treat watering eyes, wounds, and rashes. It helps promote heart and respiratory functions, because of its ability to soothe the mucous membranes that line the respiratory, digestive, and urinary tracts and helps counter infection. Most recently, it has been used to prevent morning sickness, ease liver and stomach complaints, check internal hemorrhage, increase appetite and the secretion of bile, and as a mouthwash.

Gotu Kola

Gotu Kola contains no cola or caffeine, as its name would suggest. This herb is called "brain food" by many and is viewed as one of the best herbal nerve tonics out there, as it promotes memory and as an energy enhancer; it acts to prevent aging. It is effective in treatment of mental problems dealing with anxiety and loss of memory.

Horsetail

The ancient Greeks knew of its astringent properties, and therefore is used for both internal and external wounds. Horsetail contains the highest amount of silica of all known herbs, which helps to strengthen fingernails, increases the flow of urine, and helps to hold calcium in the body. Silica is found in connective tissues throughout the body and is important in the building and repair of healthy connective tissue and in bone maintenance, enhancing bone flexibility, and adhesion aiding in circulation. In Guatemala, American Indians have used this for polyps, and abdominal and oral cancers.

Hydrangea

Originally used by the Cherokee Indians as a remedy for kidney stones, hydrangea was introduced to early American settlers for similar purposes. It increases the flow of urine and will aid in the removal of gallstones and the pain caused by them. It helps correct bedwetting in children. As a diuretic, it is particularly helpful for prostrate infection and inflammation and for kidney fluid retention. It is also effective for arthritic swelling and bladder infections.

Jasmine

This sensually sweet floral aroma has been used as an aphrodisiac for centuries. Jasmine supports the nervous system and is especially helpful for the mature woman's changing needs and dry, sensitive skin.

Jojoba

The pressed seeds of this plant produce an oil that is used extensively in the cosmetic business, especially in products for the hair and skin. A few drops lightly massaged into the hair and scalp after shampooing helps cleanse and moisturize the scalp. Jojoba also lightly coats the hair, giving it extra shine, body, and protection. Jojoba oil makes an excellent conditioning treatment.

Kava Kava

According to legend, the kava kava drinker often felt utter contentment and a greater sense of well-being. Kava kava helps reduce anxiety without impairing mental function, as it works on the central nervous system and promotes relaxation to those suffering from stress and anxiety. It is known as one of the most powerful of herbal muscle relaxants out there. It helps promote a more restful sleep in those struggling with insomnia or restlessness and it helps relax sore, tired, tense muscles.

Kelp

Kelp, commonly referred to as seaweed or "a gift from the sea," grows along coastlines around the world. It is a rich source of natural vitamins and minerals, including essential trace minerals. Kelp is a nutritional source that is used to promote healthy glandular functions, focusing especially on the thyroid. Kelp is especially high in iodine, which must be present for proper glandular function. By regulating the thyroid, Kelp helps stimulate and balance the metabolism. The large amounts of iodine found in Kelp are important in the treatment of an under-active thyroid. Consequently, Kelp may contribute to weight loss if the weight gain is directly related to thyroid disorders. Kelp helps improve digestion, stimulate kidney function, increase circulation, and purify the blood. Kelp has also been known to treat inflamed joints and tissues caused by arthritis & rheumatism. Furthermore, Kelp enhances the immune system and eliminates the negative effects that stress may have on the body.

L-Arginine

L-Arginine not only supports the body's efforts to regulate blood pressure, it enhances sexual function and boosts immune, heart and brain functions. Scientific studies have shown that taking l-arginine orally can improve the beneficial expansion of blood vessels, thereby allowing the blood to flow more freely through the cardiovascular system. This may help the body maintain blood pressure levels already within the normal range and support healthy cardiovascular and sexual function. This product also has a beneficial effect on the kidneys, helping them control salt levels in the body. Salt levels have been linked to high blood pressure.

L-Carnitine

L-Carnitine is an amino acid from which certain proteins are made. It is synthesized in the liver and kidneys. The body requires l-carnitine for the transport of long-chain fatty acids into the cells. According to the National Research Council, symptoms of carnitine deficiency include progressive muscle weakness and severe hypoglycemia.

L-Glutamine

L-Glutamine is an amino acid, a protein building block that is important in supplying the brain with energy.

L-Lysine

L-Lysine is an essential amino acid, which cannot be produced by the body and is required by the body for the manufacture of proteins. It helps ensure adequate absorption of calcium and the formation of collagen for bone, cartilage, and connective tissue. Lysine strengthens circulation and helps the immune system manufacture antibodies. It also helps control the body's acid/alkaline balance, which plays a role in cold sores, influences the pineal and mammary glands and plays a role in gallbladder function.

Lavender

Lavender's cool, mellow, peaceful fragrance has traditionally been used for its balancing effects and soothing properties. It contains antiseptic, antibacterial, antiviral, and antifungal compounds. It is an effective herb for headaches, especially when they are related to stress. Lavender can be quite effective in the clearing of depression, especially if used in conjunction with other remedies. As a gentle strengthening tonic of the nervous system, it is used in states of nervous debility and exhaustion. Known topical uses include acne, burns, cellulite, cold sores, eczema, edema, fatigue, halitosis, headache, infection, insect bites, insect repellent, insect stings, irritability, joint pain, lice, muscle soreness, rheumatism, scabies, scars, snakebites, toothache, vertigo, and yeast infections. Place a drop of Lavender essential oil on the edge of the mattress of a teething baby to calm him/her down. Use Lavender as a rinse for fragrant hair, and use it in massage oil, and as a salve for eczema.

Lecithin

It is produced daily by the liver if the diet is adequate. Lecithin is needed by every cell in the body and is a key building block of cell membranes; without it, they would harden. Lecithin protects cells from oxidation and largely comprises the protective sheaths surrounding the brain. Hence, it supports the circulatory system.

Lemon Oil

It contains antibacterial, antifungal, and antiseptic compounds. Its toning and soothing actions are helpful for skin conditions, including oily skin. Its bright aroma is stimulating, refreshing, and clean.

Licorice Root

We know this herb for its wide use as a candy flavoring, but its value goes far beyond that. The medicinal use of licorice goes back several thousand years. Licorice root has been used by traditional herbalists as a general tonic and for respiratory support. It also supports the liver. Licorice is included in most Chinese herb combinations to balance the other herbs and to promote vitality. It has a reputation for bringing the entire body into balance, particularly for women who menstruate, and promoting well-being.

Lobelia

Lobelia is used as an effective blood cleanser, and also to treat a variety of respiratory problems. As one of the most useful muscle re-laxants, Lobelia is rich in vitamin A, vitamin C, and manganese. It is used as an expectorant, expelling phlegm from the lungs, and relieving congestion that is typically related to asthma and bronchitis. Lobelia has also been known to reduce cold and flu symptoms, suppress cough-ing, and stimulate perspiration, cooling down the body to help break fevers. Lobelia is considered beneficial for treating mild depression, reducing inflammation & pain, easing muscle tension, and calming the nerves. It also acts as a mild laxative for alleviating constipation. Lobelia is often used as a tobacco substitute to help those who wish to quit smoking. Also effective in controlling epileptic seizures.

Magnesium

Seventy percent of the body's magnesium is found in the bones, and the rest is found mainly in the soft tissues and blood. Magnesium is necessary for the metabolism of vitamin C, phosphorus, potassium, and sodium. It is important to the nervous system and the synthesis of certain proteins. It governs how calcium is used in the body.

Marjoram Oil

Marjoram Pure Essential Oil has a warm and soothing aroma that calms yet strengthens. Marjoram helps relieve tense, sore muscles.

Marshmallow

Marshmallow has been utilized for thousands of years not only as a food during times of famine, but for its healing properties as an herbal remedy. Marshmallow has primarily been used for the respiratory and digestive tracts, its high mucilage content may also provide some minor relief for urinary tract and skin infections. Marshmallow's content helps soothe inflamed tissues, often caused by bronchitis and asthma. Marshmallow also relieves dryness and irritation in the chest and throat, usually brought on by colds and persistent coughs. Marshmallow has been known to relieve indigestion, kidney problems, urinary tract infections, and even external skin wounds such as boils and abscesses.

Milk Thistle

Milk thistle helps protect the liver from the toxins it collects and breaks down. It provides nutrients that must be present for the liver to perform its 500 or more functions, including filtering and destroying toxins in the body. Milk Thistle is a good supplement to use to protect the liver when needing to take pharmaceutical drugs. In the 19th century the Eclectics used the herb for varicose veins, menstrual difficulty, and congestion in the liver, spleen and kidneys.

Neroli Oil

Neroli Pure Essential Oil has a fresh, floral aroma that brightens the spirits and clears the mind. Neroli's soothing properties enhances skin tone and supports the body under stress.

Niacin

Niacin is important to both the circulatory and nervous systems. The body's energy system also requires niacin for proper function

Noni Juice

Noni juice supports several systems in the body and actually works at the cellular level. It can increase mental clarity and attention span, as well as allow greater physical performance levels. Anyone, young or old can take the juice. The benefits of noni juice are universal and may be enjoyed by all without hesitation. It supports proper digestion, helps support the immune system to help it fight off infection, is an antioxidant, and increases your energy levels. It has been a blessing in my life, to know more about my own testimonies with this product, please feel free contact me. It can benefit the following systems of the body:

Digestive System:
- Diarrhea
- Intestinal Parasites
- Indigestion
- Stomach Ulcers

Chest Infections
- Cough
- Tuberculosis
- Asthma
- Respiratory Afflictions

Internal Disorders
- Diabetes
- High Blood Pressure
- Headache /Migraines
- Depression
- Kidney and Bladder

Eye Infections
- Eye Complaints

Other disorders
- Malignancies or Tumors
- Cancer
- Epilepsy seizures

Fevers
- Fever with vomiting or Flu

Mouth and Throat Infections
- Inflamed, sore gums
- Sore throat with cough
- Thrush
- Gingivitis
- Toothache

Skin Infections and Inflammations
- Abscess
- Boil, Carbuncle
- Abrasions
- Blemishes
- Wounds, Infections

Gender Specific
- Childbirth and Pregnancy
- Menstrual Cramps
- Regulate Menstrual Flow

Papaya

Papaya nutritionally supports the digestive system. It is great for indigestion, heartburn, inflammatory bowel disorders, and appetite stimulation.

Passion Flower

Passion Flower leaves have been used traditionally as a sedative. In fact, Algonquin Indians used passion flower tea to help soothe their nerves. Passion flower supports the nervous system in a variety of ways. Many have found that it helps with relaxation of tense muscles and tension headaches. It is widely used to promote a restful night's sleep.

Patchouli Oil

This is soothing, calming, and sensuous oil that should be used sparingly. It has antibacterial, antifungal, antiseptic, and antiviral compounds and is beneficial to the skin, particularly dry skin.

Pau D'Arco

Pau D'Arco also helps build blood, supports detoxification and helps maintain a healthy circulatory system. The herb also has the ability to strengthen and support the immune system. the powdered herb has been used successfully to treat immune deficiency disorders, cardiovascular problems, and may be used to reduce blood pressure. Pau D'Arco is also considered a good blood cleanser and detoxifier. It may be used safely to treat all types of infections, stimulate urine flow, reduce fevers, and aid digestion. Pau D'Arco contains properties that are beneficial in relieving inflammation and pain related to bowel problems, ulcers, arthritis and rheumatism. Externally, Pau D'Arco has been used to treat of a variety of inflammatory skin problems & infections, including fungal infections, hemorrhoids, eczema and wounds. Pau D'Arco bark is also known to help lower blood sugar levels, and acts as a mild laxative. It is used as a support drug for lung, prostate and colon cancer, and also believed to increase red blood cell production.

Peppermint Oil

This popular flavoring has a variety of uses in herblogy. A couple of drops can be added to a glass of water or a cup of hot water for a soothing, refreshing after-meal drink as well as a digestive aid. Peppermint helps promote digestion and has cooling and stimulating properties. Many people put a touch of peppermint oil on the temples to help with a headache.

Red Clover

Herbalists have long prized this herb for it's traditional use as a blood purifier, expelling toxins from the bloodstream. Researchers from the National Cancer Institute (NCI) have found anti-cancer properties in this herb. Red Clover is one of the most useful remedies for children with skin problems. Because it is mild, it makes an excellent nutritional supplement for children. The expectorant and anti-spasmodic action give this remedy a role in the treatment of coughs and bronchitis, but especially in whooping cough, dry cough and colds. Red Clover also increases the production of mucus and urine flow helping relieve irritation and inflammation of the urinary tract. As a digestive aid, Red Clover stimulates the production of digestive fluids and bile. It also relieves constipation and helps soothe inflammation of the bowel, stomach and intestines. Red Clover contains easily absorbed calcium & magnesium which tones and relaxes the nervous system, relieving tension due to stress and the associated headaches which are further relieved by the silicic acid content. For women, Red Clover is quite special it contains stilbene which stimulates eostrogenic activity, thus increasing fertility, and reduces "hot flashes" experienced by women during menopause. It also supports the uterus with it's vitamin content, and the high protein content nourishes the whole body.

Red Raspberry

Red raspberry possesses astringent qualities, and women have used the leaves for centuries as a support to the reproductive system, especially during pregnancy. This herb helps the body control morning sickness. Studies show that it helps relax the uterus. Many find that the astringent compounds in red raspberry leaves also help alleviate diarrhea.

Rosemary Oil

This oil has antiseptic properties and a strong aroma that is balancing, invigorating, revitalizing, and regenerating. It stimulates the scalp and has been used for centuries on oily hair and skin. **Do not use during pregnancy or with those with high blood pressure or epilepsy.**

Safflowers

The oil of this plant is commonly used for cooking in the U.S. Safflowers are also a natural nutritional aid for the digestive system. Safflower blossoms are used in the tea form to treat hysteria, fevers, phlegm, and panic attacks. It is a pretty strong cathartic, and also clears the lungs and helps the phthisis. It is likewise beneficial against jaundice. An infusion of this herb stimulates the menstrual flow. Safflowers have been to relieve arthritis, treat skin rashes, and promote healthy liver functions.

Sage

A member of the mint family, sage's name comes from the Latin salvare, which means "to heal." Sage is highly astringent and aromatic. Extracts of sage have antioxidant properties; they act as a preservative, which probably explains sage's wide use as a meat seasoning for centuries. Its aromatic properties help sage create an environment that is unfriendly to foreign invaders.

Sandalwood Oil

This sensual oil is calming, balancing, and harmonizing. It contains antifungal, antiseptic, and antiviral compounds and has a balancing action on the skin.

Sarsaparilla

Sarsaparilla is considered a blood purifier, and as such, it supports the liver. It also has anti-inflammatory and tonic properties and has been used traditionally for skin ailments. It may also promote normal digestion and appetite. Sarsaparilla root is said to be good for gout, rheumatism, colds, fevers, and catarrhal problems, as well as for relieving flatulence. Sarsaparilla reduces fevers by helping cool down the body and promoting perspiration. A tea made from it has also been used externally for skin problems, scrofula, ringworm, and tetters. It also stimulates the production of reproductive hormones, and has tonic action on the sexual organs. Sarsaparilla helps to increase testosterone & progesterone levels in the body. It is said to excite the passions, making men more virile and women more sensuous.

Saw Palmetto

Saw Palmetto is used primarily to support glandular tissues (especially the prostate gland) and to balance the hormones. Saw Palmetto berries historically have been used to treat several related disorders of the genito-urinary system, including inflammation, rupture and blockage. Saw Palmetto continues to be an herb that effectively acts to tone and strengthen the male reproductive system. It may be used with safety where a boost to the male sex hormones is required, as is obviously specific in cases of enlarged prostate glands. In addition to its primary application to support prostate problems, this herb is useful for asthma and all kinds of throat troubles, colds, bronchitis, la grippe, whooping cough, and throat irritation. It is especially useful when there is excessive mucous discharge from the sinuses and nose. Saw Palmetto also strengthens the thyroid, which controls overall gland function. This herb can also reduce breast tenderness related to breast feeding and menstruation. There is evidence that Saw Palmetto may also be used to balance the metabolism, aid digestion, and stimulate appetite to increase weight gain.

Slippery Elm

It helps relieve digestive discomfort and provides mucilage to soothe the digestive tract. The herb works with the body to draw out impurities and toxins, assisting with the healing of all body parts. Slippery Elm's coating action soothes the irritated tissues of the intestines, colon, urinary tract, and stomach ulcers. Slippery Elm is also beneficial in alleviating inflammation caused by arthritis, and for soothing sore throats.

Spirulina

Spirulina is a blue-green algae that grows in warm, alkaline fresh waters around the world. The algae is a source of all eight essential amino acids, as well as chelated minerals, natural plant sugars, trace minerals, and enzymes. Spirulina is easily assimilated by the body.

St. John's Wort

St. John's Wort is known for its benefits to the nervous system, specifically for help with mild to moderate depression. It supports emotional balance and a feeling of well-being. St. John's Wort helps maintain a positive outlook and healthy motivation.

Tea Tree Oil

Tea Tree Oil has been referred to as "the wonder from Down Under." Tea Tree has long been used for its antibacterial, antifungal, antiseptic, and antiviral properties.

Uva Ursi

Uva Ursi leaf is widely used as a diuretic, astringent, and antiseptic. Folk medicine around the world has recommended Uva Ursi for nephritis, kidney stones, and chronic cystitis. The herb has also been used as a general tonic for weakened kidneys, liver or pancreas. Uva Ursi works best when one avoids acidic foods, such as citrus fruits & juices, cranberry products, sauerkraut, and vitamin C. This herb helps prevent postpartum infection. Uva Ursi is also helpful for chronic diarrhea. As a nutritional supplement and muscle relaxant, Uva Ursi soothes, strengthens, and tightens irritated & inflamed tissues.

Valerian Root

Valerian for a host of medical problems, including digestive problems, nausea, liver problems, and even urinary tract disorders. Use of Valerian for insomnia and nervous conditions has been common for many centuries. Valerian was traditionally used for epilepsy, sleeplessness, nervousness, hysteria, and as a diuretic.

Wild Yam

Wild Yam has been used for centuries by women seeking nutritional support and optimal balance for the glandular system. In herbal medicine, Wild Yam is a remedy that can be used to relieve intestinal colic, soothe diverticulitis, and ease dysmenorrhea, ovarian & uterine pain, as listed by the British Herbal Pharmacopoeia. It is also of great use in the treatment of rheumatoid arthritis, especially the acute phase where there is intense inflammation. Traditional herbalists have recommended this herb for bilious colic, colic with spasmodic contractions, yellow skin & conjunctiva, abdominal pain, and stomach problems. This herb can reduce menstrual cramping, relieve some symptoms related to menopause, decrease water retention, and alleviates nausea caused by pregnancy. Wild Yam's antispasmodic properties relax muscles and help reduce inflammations. Wild Yam is also beneficial in treating arthritis, rheumatism and muscle spasms. Other uses for Wild Yam include easing digestion, by dilating vessels and stimulating bile flow, and contributing to the reduction of cholesterol and blood pressure levels.

Yarrow

Yarrow is known to alleviate inflammation, reduce fevers, stimulate the appetite, and encourage sweating, thus expelling toxins from the body. Yarrow's astringent properties are especially helpful in stopping nosebleeds, excessive menstruation, and diarrhea. Yarrow is also known for relieving muscle spasms, arthritis, and easing digestion.

Yellow Dock

Yellow Dock, a member of the buckwheat family, grows abundantly throughout the US. Pioneers used it for nutritional support of the urinary system. Yellow dock promotes proper elimination and colon health. It also supports liver function.

Yucca

Yucca supports structural health because of its influence on joint health and function. The plant provides powerful nutritional support to the structural system. Yucca contains antibacterial and anti-fungal properties that contribute to cleansing of the colon, purifying of the blood, and helping to keep the kidneys & liver free of toxins. Yucca is used today to treat inflammations caused by degenerative diseases like arthritis and rheumatism and it is also good for dandruff and hair loss.

Zinc

This trace mineral is extremely important to overall health. More zinc is found in the body than any other trace element except for iron. Relatively large amounts are found in bone and muscle, and it is also prevalent in the prostate and retina. Zinc is involved in sugar metabolism and seems to be easily lost from the system. Pregnant and lactating women require extra zinc.

HERBS RECOMMENDED DURING PREGNANCY

Many herbs are helpful during pregnancy, especially just before childbirth. Use these herbs in the gentlest way as hot relaxing teas, capsules, or tinctures. The following herbs **ARE RECOMMENDED** during one's pregnancy, as they can alleviate nausea, morning sickness, pain and the like.

- **Bilberry:** fortifies vein and capillary support, aids in kidney function and is a mild diuretic for bloating.
- **Blue Cohosh:** stops and eliminates false labor pains, can be used for final weeks of pregnancy to ease and / or induce labor.
- **Burdock Root:** helps prevent water retention and jaundice in the baby.
- **Chamomile:** aids digestive and bowel problems and relaxes for good sleep.
- **Echinacea:** aids the immune system to prevent colds, flu, and infections.
- **Ginger Root:** excellent for morning sickness
- **Lobelia:** helps to relax the mother during delivery and helps to speed up the delivery of the placenta.
- **Nettles:** guards against excessive bleeding as it has vitamin K in it; improves kidney function and helps prevent hemorrhoids.
- **Peppermint:** after the first trimester, may be used to help digestion, soothe the stomach, and overcome nausea. It is an overall body strengthener and cleanser.
- **Red Raspberry:** all-around excellent herb to use for pregnancy. It is a uterine tonic, anti-abortive and helps prevent infection.

It aids in preventing cramps and anemia and prevents excessive bleeding during and after labor and will facilitate the birth process by stimulating contractions.

ભ **Wild Yam**: eases pregnancy pain, nausea or cramping and will lessen the risk of miscarriage.

ભ **Yellow Dock**: aids in iron assimilation and helps to prevent infant jaundice.

THE FOLLOWING HERBS ARE *NOT RECOMMENDED* TO BE TAKEN DURING YOUR PREGNANCY:

ભ **Angelica**: can cause uterine contractions.

ભ **Black Cohosh**: use only in final weeks of pregnancy, as it will induce labor.

ભ **Coffee**: irritates the uterus, and excessive amounts in some sensitive individuals can cause premature birth or miscarriage.

ભ **Eucalyptus Oil**: avoid during pregnancy, as it is difficult to eliminate through the kidneys.

ભ **False unicorn**: use only in the final weeks of pregnancy, as it will induce labor.

ભ **Golden Seal**: large amounts can cause uterine contractions.

ભ **Juniper**: causes a too strong vaso-dilating, diuretic effect.

ભ **Ma Huang (ephedra):** avoid because of strong of an antihistamine effect.

ભ **Mistletoe**: can cause uterine contractions.

ભ **Pennyroyal**: can cause abortion.

ભ **Wild Ginger**: can cause uterine contractions.

ભ **Yarrow**: a strong astringent and mild abortifacient.

THE FOLLOWING HERBS ARE LAXATIVE IN NATURE AND SHOULD BE USED SPARINGLY OR IN COMBINATIONS:

Aloe Vera	Barberry	Buckthorn
Cascara	Sagrada	Mandrake
Rhubarb	Senna	

HERBAL SUGGESTIONS FOR COMMON HEALTH CONDITIONS

- **Acne**
  Aloe vera gel, alfalfa, echinacea, dandelion root, chaparral, lemon, patchouli, rosewood, sandalwood, tea tree oil, ylang ylang
- **Arthritis**
  Alfalfa, comfrey, black cohosh, valerian root, burdock root, skullcap, cayenne, sarsaparilla
- **Asthma**
  Chickweed, chamomile, comfrey, fenugreek, licorice root, ginger, horsetail
- **Bad Breath**
  Chlorophyll, peppermint, rosemary, sage, myrrh
- **Blood Pressure – HIGH**
  Cayenne, garlic, black cohosh, gotu kola, myrrh, kelp
- **Blood Pressure – LOW**
  Parsley, dandelion, golden seal root, ginger, garlic, ginseng
- **Blood Purifier**
  Red clover, burdock, garlic, dandelion, licorice, echinacea, chaparral, sarsaparilla, comfrey, lemon.
- **Bronchitis**
  Ginger, golden seal, comfrey, myrrh, chickweed
- **Cancer**
  Echinacea, noni Juice, red clover, burdock, golden seal, parsley, comfrey, pau d'arco, chickweed, chlorophyll, bee pollen
- **Circulation**
  Cayenne, garlic, ginger, black cohosh, comfrey, horseradish
- **Cholesterol**
  Cayenne, garlic, kelp, black cohosh, golden seal
- **Colon Cleansing/Laxative**
  Red clover, ginger, chlorophyll, cascara sagrada, garlic, cayenne, coffee enemas

ભ **Depression**
Gotu kola, St. John's Wort, kelp, ginger, basil, noni juice

ભ **Diabetes**
Ginseng, spirulina, garlic, parsley, golden seal, kelp, licorice, juniper

ભ **Diarrhea**
Comfrey, bayberry, red raspberry, chamomile, kelp

ભ **Digestion**
Papaya, ginger root, catnip, comfrey, safflower, cayenne, noni juice dandelion

ભ **Ear Aches**
Warm olive oil, warm garlic oil, hydrogen peroxide, ear candles

ભ **Energy**
Licorice, siberian ginseng, ginger root, garlic, gotu kola, kelp, bee pollen

ભ **Epilepsy**
Lobelia, scullcap, catnip tea, milk thistle, calcium/magnesium, siberian ginseng, noni juice.

ભ **Eyes**
Golden seal, red raspberry, alfalfa, spirulina, noni juice

ભ **Fasting**
Licorice root, spirulina, bee pollen

ભ **Female Problems**
Ginger, marshmallow, red raspberry, golden seal, black cohosh, lobelia, dong quai

ભ **Fever**
Peppermint, valerian, dandelion, chamomile, lobelia, fenugreek,

ભ **Fingernails – strengthen**
Horsetail, comfrey, kelp, alfalfa, chlorophyll, spirulina

ભ **Food Poisoning**
Charcoal tablets, alfalfa, kelp, fennel, lobelia tea

ભ **Gallbladder**
Horsetail, dandelion, parsley, peppermint, ginger root, red clover, golden seal, garlic

ⅭⅯ **Glands**
Garlic, Siberian ginseng, black cohosh, licorice root, mullein, lobelia, kelp, saw palmetto berries, alfalfa, echinacea

ⅭⅯ **Gums**
Comfrey, peppermint, lobelia, cloves, golden seal, baking soda

ⅭⅯ **Hair**
Alfalfa, sage, rosemary, spirulina, kelp

ⅭⅯ **Hay fever**
Comfrey, parsley, lobelia, chaparral, burdock, marshmallow, bee pollen

ⅭⅯ **Headache**
Ginger, valerian, peppermint, thyme, rosemary, white willow bark, basil, ephedra, noni juice

ⅭⅯ **Heart Problems**
Hawthorn berries, cayenne, garlic, ginseng, lecithin, rosemary, blue cohosh, dandelion, valerian root, evening primrose, kelp

ⅭⅯ **Hemorrhoids**
Bee pollen, comfrey, parsley, aloe vera, myrrh, burdock, uva ursi, cayenne, garlic

ⅭⅯ **Hypoglycemia**
Spirulina, bee pollen, royal jelly, licorice root, Siberian ginseng, ginger, gotu kola, safflower, cayenne, uva ursi, noni juice

ⅭⅯ **Immune System**
Echinacea, Siberian ginseng, golden seal, myrrh, yarrow, cayenne, garlic, spirulina, bee pollen

ⅭⅯ **Indigestion**
Peppermint tea, comfrey, ginseng, chamomile, fennel, papaya

ⅭⅯ **Insomnia**
Valerian, scullcap, catnip, passion flower

ⅭⅯ **Kidney Problems**
Uva ursi, juniper berries, parsley, marshmallow root, alfalfa, ginger, chamomile, noni juice

ⅭⅯ **Liver**
Dandelion, goldenrod, lobelia, parsley, comfrey, wild yam, carrot juice

ભ **Longevity**
Bee pollen, spirulina, ginseng, gotu kola, licorice, cayenne, garlic

ભ **Lungs**
Slippery elm, bayberry bark, chickweed, ginseng, marshmallow, lobelia, comfrey

ભ **Memory**
Gotu kola, ginseng, rosemary, chlorophyll, alfalfa, bee pollen, lecithin, gingko/gotu kola

ભ **Menopause**
Kelp, sage, black Cohosh, damiana, red raspberry, ginseng, sarsaparilla, licorice

ભ **Menstrual Cramps**
Red raspberry, dong quai, chamomile, wild yam, kelp, black cohosh, blue cohosh, alfalfa, evening primrose oil, peppermint tea

ભ **Muscle Cramps**
Alfalfa, chlorophyll, kelp, blue cohosh, dong quai, spirulina, horsetail, saffron (or eat a banana for to increase potassium levels)

ભ **Nerves**
Valerian root, rosemary, passion flower, mistletoe, agrimony, scullcap, white willow bark, ginger

ભ **Osteoporosis**
Kelp, horsetail, alfalfa, oat straw

ભ **Pain**
Chamomile, catnip, mullein, valerian, cayenne, white willow bark, scullcap, kelp, blue vervain, wild yam

ભ **Pancreas**
Juniper berries, mullein, comfrey, garlic, yarrow, golden seal, licorice, uva ursi, cayenne, dandelion

ભ **Poison Oak/Ivy**
Black walnut extract, aloe vera gel, mugwort, echinacea

ભ **Prostrate**
Parsley, saw palmetto, juniper berries, gotu kola, horsetail, kelp, golden seal, uva ursi, bee pollen, lecithin

ભ **Senility**
Gotu kola, Siberian ginseng, cayenne, alfalfa, kelp, peppermint, scullcap, lecithin

ભ **Stress/Tension**
Valerian root, spearmint, chamomile, catnip, peppermint, passion flower, rosemary, scullcap, lobelia, bee pollen

ભ **Thyroid**
Golden seal, kelp, cayenne, black cohosh, parsley, iodine, black walnut, sarsaparilla

ભ **Tumors/Cysts**
Echinacea, Oregon grape, dandelion, red clover, golden seal, comfrey, yellow dock, slippery elm, kelp, evening primrose oil, chickweed

ભ **Ulcers**
Cayenne, slippery elm, myrrh, licorice, golden seal, comfrey, alfalfa, sage, chickweed, aloe vera juice

ભ **Weight Reduction**
Spirulina, alfalfa, chickweed lecithin, licorice, kelp, iodine, burdock, black walnut, papaya

ભ **Worms/Parasites**
Black walnut, garlic, chaparral, sage

ભ **Yeast Infection**
Golden seal, myrrh, witch hazel, comfrey, garlic, juniper berries

The statements on this page have not been evaluated by the FDA. These products are not meant to diagnose, treat, cure or prevent any disease.

Recommended Reading:

The Little Herb Encyclopedia by Jack Ritchason, ND
Healthy Healing, an alternative healing reference by Linda Rector-Page, ND, PHD
Healing With Herbs and Home Remedies A-Z by Hanna Kroeger

Chapter Eleven

水

Feng Shui and How it Can Impact Your Life

Feng Shui is an expression in the Cantonese dialect of the Chinese language and simply means "wind" (feng) and "water" (shui). Although it is pronounced in different ways depending on the Chinese dialect, the commonly pronounced "Fung Schway" seems to be the most widely used pronunciation in the Western world. It has to do with arranging a room to make us feel good. Feng Shui does create wonderful living and workspaces; however, it also enhances our life by creating greater harmony and balance. It has been described as the "Science of Common Sense." It has also been stated that Feng Shui teaches us "what we already know to be true." Those that have applied Feng Shui principles have described their lives (and businesses) as "miraculously transformed." Robert Redford, Steven Spielberg, Donald Trump, Deepak Chopra, are among the many users of Feng Shui. Some buildings and corporations that have had feng shui principles applied to them are Avalon Towers in San Francisco, Trump Tower in New York City, MGM Grand Hotel in Las Vegas, White Sox Stadium in Aveda, Hyatt Hotel in Singapore, Chase Manhattan's Merchant Bank in Hong Kong and soon to open Hong Kong's Disneyland.

WHAT IS FENG SHUI?
Feng Shui is an ancient environmental art/science, more than 4,000 years old, that provides environmental tools to adjust the flow

of energy or chi in a space to produce positive and beneficial results in our lives. Understanding this ancient art of placement is an important step towards improving your life and health. When Feng Shui principles are applied, we not only see results, we feel the difference, and on a deeper level, we experience the change through life situation improvements. The information provided in this chapter is to simply acquaint you with this fascinating art/science and direct you towards an improved lifestyle. Feng Shui balance helps to create wholeness, abundance, spiritual growth, and joy in your life. Before we go any further, let me tell you that it is working right now! Take a look at the space you are in at the moment and consider the things that you see. Is the area dark or light, cold or warm, confusing or tranquil, clean or dirty, spacious and organized or cluttered? Your answers will describe the way energy is moving in that space.

The earliest method of Feng Shui was called the Landform or Form School. This approach to Feng Shui utilizes information about local conditions and the observation of these conditions. Buildings could be constructed in such a way that provided the best protection from prevailing winds and waterways. The Compass approach relies on information from environmental conditions and direction. A compass or an instrument called a luo pan is used. Additionally, astronomy and astrology has significance in interpreting proper location and placement.

Intuitive Feng Shui is based in applying the sensibilities of the people residing in and working with the land and water areas. This approach honors the intuitive skills of the people and their working knowledge of the area that was to be built upon. These instincts developed through their personal experience with their environment, working with the land, and in growing crops. Remember that Feng Shui is about change and its principles are fluid, not rigid. The key to understanding the principles is found when you are empowered by the information to create sacred, harmonious spaces, removed from fear-based concepts. The amazing thing about Feng Shui is that all approaches work!

DO I HAVE TO HAVE CERTAIN BELIEFS ?

Since Feng Shui is NOT a religion, it does not require a belief system to be effective. We can say it has a lot to do with the study of mundane and etheric energy or life force called chi (pronounced chee). Unless you are into quantum physics, which is the theory in physics based on the concept of the subdivision of radiant energy into definite amounts, then the answer to "How does it work?" may be boring. And if you had to understand how your TV works in order to watch it, then I guess you would miss some great shows.

HOW DO WE BEGIN OUR FENG SHUI JOURNEY?

First Step: Declutter, Declutter, Declutter!! In ancient times, this may not have been a vital first step since lifestyles were not inundated with the accumulation of material possessions. Yes, there were displays of wealth but not like our modern society's industrial and technological society production of the abundance of "stuff." As a result of attachment to possessions, an abundance of material stuff is produced and therefore, our society suffers from a disease process called "I need more!" An important "first step" on the jolly Feng Shui trail is to declutter! This is vital! Clutter produces slow moving and eventually stagnant energy in the space it occupies. This "stuck energy" literally makes you feel stuck resulting in negative events in your life. Think about how wonderful it feels to have a space cleared of all the clutter and cleaned. It is a big lift to your spirit, energy is flowing again, the space feels lighter, looks brighter, you feel better. The goal of Feng Shui is to produce an indoor and outdoor environment that nourishes you.

CLUTTER FALLS INTO THESE CATEGORIES:

Things unloved, unwanted, not needed, needing repair, kept because you'd feel guilty if you got rid of it (that never used fondue set Aunt Tillie gave you), things kept "just in case" you may need it, unfinished projects, and things disorganized and untidy. Remember that "out of order" means "not working." We want our life and health to be in good working order!! Feng Shui metaphorically demonstrates to you to the connection between the space you occupy and the events in your life. As your awareness of your environment increases, you begin to "see" that your home is an outward expression of what is going on inside you. Feeling "stuck" in your approach to life? Review your entrance to your home and see if any "clutter" is broadcasting that message. By releasing those possessions that no longer serve you, you are letting go of the old and creating space for the new. The decluttering process is an extremely revealing method that allows you to learn about you and your attachment to the physical plane.

A way to reveal this connection between your life situation and the space you occupy is through using a wonderful tool called a Bagua. The Feng Shui Bagua is an octagonal shape diagram used for providing insight to our life situation. This eight-sided octagon map is based on the Chinese oracle of the I-Ching (pronounced eee-ching), called the Bagua (pronounced bah gwah). Translated, it means "eight trigrams." Each section or zone is called a "gua." These eight sides along with the center make up the nine categories of life. Every environment can be divided into nine sections, each with a corresponding symbolic meaning to a specific area of our life.

THE BAGUA

prosperity	fame and reputation	relationships and love
family	health	creativity and children
skills and knowledge	career	helpful people and travel

THESE LIFE STATIONS OF THE BAGUA ARE:

Fame and Reputation — focuses on reputation, accomplishments, integrity, and character, how you view yourself.

Love and Relationships — relationships with significant others, relationships with colleagues and friends, developing cooperation with all relationships.

Children and Creativity — mental clarity, inspiration, motivation, enthusiasm, creativity, children.

Helpful People and Travel — clients, mentors, people giving you referrals, assistants, synchronicity, and travel.

Life Path and Career — life purpose and mission, our life's journey.

Skills and Knowledge — personal growth, enlightenment, spirituality, education, wisdom, serenity.

Family and Health — Specific health issues, family relationships/issues.

Prosperity/Wealth — abundance and gratitude.

Center — General Health /Wellness — total spiritual and physical health and well-being, balance, harmony.

It is within these physical sections of a space where you can determine how energy is flowing. Allow yourself to observe these spaces and see what you desire to change and improve.

By laying the bagua over a floor plan and placing the front three guas along the wall where the formal front door entrance is placed, we establish the various life stations represented in our environment. This alignment is the easiest way to use the Bagua 'map' and is used by many schools of Feng Shui. Each section of the Bagua is interconnected with all the others. In order to establish the balance of energy flowing through these spaces it is important to pay attention to all areas. Feng Shui reveals the things you see, such as water, and the things you don't, such as wind.

A common expression among Feng Shui practitioners is "There is no hiding in Feng Shui!" Clutter, seen and unseen, will affect you. So if you move your clutter to the basement, attic, or storage shed, it still occupies your space and will continue to block the flow of life enhancing energy. Once you have accurately placed the Bagua map on the floor plan of your house, office, or room, you can determine the areas of your life that require the most attention. You now have a powerful tool to make choices. These choices or "intentions" will create the supportive environment you seek. You now begin to aspire to reach your "highest authentic self."

In addition to your personal inquiry and self-discovery of Feng Shui, you may want to obtain the help from a professional Feng Shui practitioner. A consultant can review your home/office through what is called a Feng Shui audit, usually conducted on an hourly basis with rates varying on the area and expertise of the consultant. Most consultations take from one to two hours and up, depending on the size of the space. They may provide you with a written report along with the necessary adjustments that can be made to correct energy flow. They may want to obtain construction dates, previous owner's history, and previous use of the land prior to construction of the building. Your experience will depend on your practitioner, your expectations, and previous conversations with that person. A consultation is beneficial when you are buying or selling your home or business, building a home or business or doing any kind of remodeling, when your life and business need improving, for any stay in the hospital requiring use of a hospital room, preferably private, or if your general well-being needs improvement.

Workshops and seminars are conducted by professionals at reasonable prices and can provide more "hands on" working knowledge. At these workshops, you will learn about the physical world and our connection to it, the history of Feng Shui, use of colors, fragrance, numbers, shapes, the elements (wood, fire, earth, water, and metal), adjustments called "Cures," directions, symbols, and most importantly "thought, emotion, and intention." Feng Shui can be applied in any space to shift the energy to a healthier vibration! It is now being embraced by some medical, dental, and other health-related facilities to provide the optimum environment for healing to occur. Most of the changes are very inexpensive and non-invasive, and will usually involve using items you already own. Our home whispers what is going on in our life. What do you want it to say? Feng Shui will allow it to communicate a positively beautiful message!

HERE ARE SOME FENG SHUI TIPS YOU CAN DO ON YOUR OWN:

1. Declutter, clean, and organize a space, and it will automatically create an energized, wonderful "feeling." I feel that this is one of the most important beginnings to balancing the energy of a space. Remember, Feng Shui is about movement and change. Just as our bodies are designed to eliminate toxins and waste,

we too should do the same in our "larger body" home. When you eliminate clutter, it will help you achieve maximum results of any feng shui placement. Now you know why it feels so wonderful to clean out your closet. You are moving the energy and revitalizing space!

2. Sleep or sit with a solid wall behind your back to ensure that you have support in your life. If the head of your bed is under a window, try rearranging it so that you have a solid wall behind you. Arrange the bed in such a way that you will have view of the bedroom door but do not place it directly in front of the door, especially where the foot of the bed lined up with the door.

3. How long have you been sleeping on those pillows? What's their condition? Remember to invest in yourself; your head and body deserve to rest upon a comfortable, clean support. Is your mattress providing this, as well? It is a good idea to place pillows sealed in a protective zippered case designed to prevent dust bunnies. Mattress protectors are also available. You can purchase these items at any linen store or from places that sell allergy relief products.

4. If you are having difficulty sleeping, make an inspection of your bedroom. At night, cover any mirrors present in the bedroom with a sheet or cloth. Remove the cloth in the daytime if you need to use the mirror. Do this for a few days and see if you feel the difference. Notice any improvements in your sleep. Many people immediately feel more relaxed and calmer upon covering or removing the bedroom mirrors.

5. In your office, have your desk positioned where it is not at the main door opening into your desk. The energy (chi) coming in will hit directly at you causing confusion, obstacles and problems. It's best to reorganize the space and place the desk facing the door but not directly in front of it. Notice how much calmer you feel when the desk is not directly in front of the door.

6. Regarding the position of your desk, avoid having your back facing the door. If there is no other placement, then place a mirror on the wall in front of you or attached to the top of your computer screen. Those round mirrors that are designed to be

attached to the side view mirrors of cars work great. You can find them in the automotive products section in the grocery store. You can also use this kind of mirror if your kitchen stove faces a wall.

7. Placement of a beautiful fish aquarium within the wealth/ prosperity area is one of the best feng shui enhancements for great results and success. Keep the aquarium clean and with fresh water. The colors purple, red, green, and gold are a perfect energy booster for this area.

8. Set out a bowl of fresh fruit on your kitchen table or snack bar and a vase of fresh flowers on a table — easy feng shui pick-me-uppers! Do not forget to eat the healthy fruit and smell the flowers!

9. Placing flowers at each side of the entrance to your home or office or along the path raises the spirits of all those that enter. Think about how nice it is when you are greeted by beautiful flowers as you are approaching someone's home.

10. Apply aromatherapy to your home — natural fragrances lift our energy and assist in purifying the air. Good quality essential oils can be found at most any health food store. Lavender oil or lemon oil drops added to a glass atomizer of water is effective when sprayed. It smells wonderful!

11. Keep your toilet lids closed when not in use.

12. Remove any ailing or dead plants from your home, office, and garden.

13. Take the TV out of the master bedroom. This seems to bring about a big protest by many, especially men. If you are not ready to part with your bedroom TV, then try to keep it in a cabinet with doors to close it off when not in use.

14. Beautiful music is a powerful mood enhancer. Get out some of your favorite tunes and remind your spirit that it can dance and sing.....and as a popular saying goes.....as if no one is watching! Music is my favorite Chi lifter. Classical, Jazz, Salsa, Beach Boys music — get the body's vibration "feeling good!"

15. Use art to upgrade the chi. Art has the ability to influence a change in your mood. Are your art choices depicting uplifting thoughts, feelings, and energy? Does it have a positive mean-

ing for you? Our home and office spaces should have art that expresses life- affirming ideals and connection.

16. Create a "sacred spot" where you can retreat and meditate on higher thoughts. You can set up a small personal "altar" on a table where you can place items like fresh flowers, pictures, candles and books, items that hold sacred meaning to you. Visit this place daily to reflect on that particular moment of your life.

17. To encourage chi toward your front door, "the mouth of chi," hang a wind chime outside and place a beautiful welcome mat by the front door. You can also feature a beautiful container of flowers, a statue you like or an animal statue like a turtle, frog, or anything that enjoys water. Water fountains and birdbaths (kept clean) are great chi invitations. If possible and it works well with your exterior color, paint your front door a healthy red.

18. If your neighbors are noisy and/or could improve the conditions of their yard and home, place a small mirror facing toward the problem house. Position it in such a way that reflects the disturbing energy away from you and back towards them. Be sure to send with it loving thoughts and a desire that they mow their grass, get rid of garbage, paint their house a pleasant shade, be peaceful. . .whatever needs to be corrected.

19. Make a "money jar" for the prosperity area of your home. Take a beautiful vase or container (purple, red, gold, and/or green are great colors to use) and place it in this decluttered zone of your home, room, and office. Inside the container, place gold (chocolate) coins, real money, a picture of something that represents abundance to you. A 100 GRAND candy bar could be one of your choices! Keep in mind that abundance and prosperity is not just about money. Our friends, family, health, and current material possessions are part of our prosperity. It is important to have gratitude for all these blessings. Write on a piece of paper (purple paper if you want or in purple ink): *"I am grateful for my abundant life filled with many blessings."* Place this affirmative note in your vase.

20. Dried flowers do not stimulate chi…it is best to have silk or fresh. Potpourri that has lost its scent no longer has chi-enhancing qualities. If you have potpourri, make sure it is a mix of natural components and refreshed weekly with good quality essential oil fragrances.

21. *The most important tip!* Move the energy of Thought and Feelings! Feelings are generated from thoughts, and since you are the commander of your thoughts, you control your feelings! So allow your thoughts to rehearse daily, moment-by-moment, positive statements about you, your life, and anything that happens in your life. Feed your mind powerful affirming messages by reading empowering books from authors that encourage you to take notice of the wonderful spirit that you are. You may want to read life-affirming works from authors such as Wayne Dyer, Lois Tschetter Hjelmstad, Robert Burney, Deepak Chopra, M.D., Marianne Williamson, James Redfield, Stuart Wilde, and others.

Instead of saying "I feel miserable" say "I am thankful to be alive," "My body has the marvelous ability and intelligence to heal," "I love my life," "I am peaceful, " and "I am an instrument of peace." This may seem awkward at first. Practice thinking and speaking empowering thoughts and it will raise the low, slow frequencies of negative thinking. A wonderful book to begin this process is *Forgive For Good* by Dr. Fred Luskin. Forgiveness starts the mind thinking in a higher spiritual pattern and begins the healing process. Transforming our thoughts is the most powerful Feng Shui enhancement we can apply!

22. YOUR BUDDHA BUDDY In order to create an environment of contentment and peace in your home place a Buddha statue in your home. Buddha will remind you about balancing your life in all ways to be truly happy, as his face expresses. He will also remind you to balance work and play and become charitable. Put him in a raised position, never on the floor. He will remind you of your own inner strength and joy.

23. THREE LEGGED TOAD OR MOON FROG Place a statue of a three legged toad (or moon frog) near (but not directly

in front of) your front door to bring wealth and prosperity into your home. He is usually holding a coin and some people recommend removing his coin in the evening and replacing it back in the day. Direct him to where he is looking towards the inside of your home, directing abundance towards you.

24. MIRRORS. Long narrow corridors create bad health because they squeeze the chi (energy) and create tension, leading to stressful quarrels and diversion. Hang a mirrors in a long narrow corridor (chi is squeezed leading to tension and quarrels —stressful conditions that affect your health. A mirror will energize and expand the area. Chi rushes quickly, like a river rapid, in a long hallway. A mirror will slow it down.

25. BEADED OR FABRIC CURTAIN. A room at the end of a long narrow hallway is considered to be in the "dragon's mouth" and not a very safe place to be. Unstable energy is produced from this and could produce illness and things happening which are out of your control. So hang an attractive bead or fabric curtain to slow the fast moving Chi.

26. CRYSTALS/MIRRORS. If you can see into your back yard, upon entering your front door your money comes in and goes right out. This is cured by hanging a faceted crystal ball between the front door and the window or door that is in the back of the house. Another choice is to place a small mirror one-inch square. on the back window frame or back door. This will keep the energy in the house. The idea is to keep the chi or energy from escaping your home before it blesses it.

27. PLANTS, WIND CHIMES (FOR THE HEALTH OF YOUR BANK ACCOUNT. If the Bagua is placed over the entire house and/or a room plan and it shows the kitchen, laundry, bathroom, toilet, or kitchen in the wealth/prosperity area, it would be considered that the money coming into that particular environment would disappear rapidly or "going down the drain." Not healthy for your bank account! To correct this situation, use either a round leaf plant, a jade plant is an excellent choice, a hanging crystal, a wind chime , a fish windsock (for the prosperity area of your back yard) and/or the colors purple, red, blue or green (the wealth colors.) Place Chinese gold

coins, wrapped in red, underneath the plant. This will symbolize the growth of your money. Use these remedies according to
your individual needs and personal aesthetics.

Recommended Readings:
Move Your Stuff, Change Your Life by Karen Rauch Carter.
Clear Your Clutter with Feng Shui by Karen Kingston.
*The Western Guide to Feng Shui: Creating Balance, Harmony, and
    Prosperity in Your Environment* by Terah Kathryn Collins
101 Ways Feng Shui Can Change Your Life by Nancilee Wydra

Chapter Twelve

Natural Alternatives For Your Health and Well-Being

We have only covered a handful of natural holistic techniques in depth in this book. There are many other great alternatives out there and I am going to try to touch on a few in this chapter.

We need to expand our horizons and understanding about health care. There is so much more to healing than just a lab test or the newest "cure-all" drug. Drugs are dealing only with symptoms, not the cause or core of the problem. They are good for short-term methods and emergencies, but taken long term they will overpower your body's natural immune response and can damage other organs in the process. In the natural holistic field of health, alternative healers and practioneers recognize that pain is the body's way of informing you that we are doing something wrong that our body does not like. Are we eating too much, or the wrong foods, are we taking on too much stress and not enough relaxation time in our lives? Pain can actually be your friend, as it is trying to tell you something is not balanced.

Alternative health care emphasizes prevention over crisis intervention, seeking to improve health rather than simply expand life by heroic means. Holistic practitioners believe healing begins within the body, not from taking medicines or having surgeries. The various fields include naturopathy, chiropractic, biofeedback, reflexology, magnet therapy, and acupuncture.

TERMS ASSOCIATED WITH HOLISTIC MEDICINE

Alternative Medicine is often used to refer to medical techniques, which are not known or accepted, by the majority "conventional" medical practitioners (usually MDs), but what is currently accepted is quickly changing. Therefore, techniques that are now considered part of Alternative Medicine will soon be considered part of "conventional" medicine. The terms Holistic Healing and Holistic Medicine are slightly more stable than Alternative Medicine and are therefore preferable. Such techniques could include non-invasive, non-pharmaceutical techniques such as Acupuncture, Homeopathy, Reiki, and many others.

Complementary Medicine is often used by conventional medical practitioners to refer to non-invasive, non-pharmaceutical techniques used as a complement to conventional medical treatments such as drugs and surgery. Also known as CAM, complementary and alternative medicine, the term implies that conventional medicine is used as a primary tool and the non-invasive, non-pharmaceutical techniques are used as a supplement when needed, such as the use of water therapy. In many cases, properly chosen non-invasive and non-pharmaceutical healing techniques, plus properly chosen lifestyle changes, can completely and safely heal both acute and chronic illnesses.

Natural Healing usually refers to the use of non-invasive and non-pharmaceutical techniques to help heal the patient. When most people use the term Natural Healing, they are usually referring to physical healing techniques only.

Acupuncture is an Oriental technique which stimulates the release of blocked energy on various points on the body using hair thin needles. Acupuncture's main use is in treating chronic and painful conditions such as arthritis, headaches, and migraines. The ancient Chinese hypothesized that energy circulated in the body via specific channels, which they called meridians. Each meridian refers to a particular organ, and the energy flowing through that meridian can be taken as indicating the functional state of that organ. Along with the usual method of puncturing the skin with the fine needles, the practitioners also use heat, pressure, friction, suction, or impulses of electromagnetic energy to stimulate the points. The acupoints are stimulated to balance the movement of energy (qi) in the body to restore health.

Applied Kinesiology is the systematic approach to patient evaluation and treatment utilizing muscle testing. Using gentle pressure, a practioneer will test the muscle strength to identify health problems and nutritional deficiencies. After diagnosis, treatment may involve exercises to strengthen a muscle, hands-on manipulation of the muscles and bones, and vitamin or mineral supplements. Practitioners analyze muscle function, posture, gait, and other structural factors in addition to inquiring about lifestyle factors that may be contributing to a health-related problem. One can learn to muscle test for themselves too, which allows you control over what you eat and drink every day and a better handle on the supplements you take on a daily basis. Muscle testing was one of the keys I learned to get a better control on my life, diet, and overall health.

Biofeedback is a training technique in which people are taught to improve their health and performance by using signals from their own bodies. One commonly used device, for example, picks up electrical signals from the muscles, and translates the signals into a form that people can detect. This device triggers a flashing light or activates a beeper every time muscles become tenser. Through clinical research and application, biofeedback techniques have expanded into widely used procedures that treat an ever-lengthening list of conditions, which include migraine headaches, tension headaches, and many other types of chronic pain disorders of the digestive system incontinence, high blood pressure, cardiac arrhythmias (abnormalities in the rhythm of the heartbeat), ADD/ADHD, Reynard's disease, epilepsy, paralysis, spinal cord injury and other movement disorders.

Chiropractic medicine operates on the theory that the improper alignment of the vertebrae (there are twenty-four vertebrae that make up the spinal column) and the spinal cord they protect, is the cause of diseases and disorders. Chiropractors apply pressure in a specific manner to allow the vertebrae in the spinal column to realign themselves. It is a physical manipulation and adjustment of the spine to relieve pain, and reduce stress in order to balance the mind, body, and spirit. Many give special attention to the physiological and biochemical aspects of the patient, including structural, spinal, musculoskeletal, neurological, vascular, nutritional, emotional, and environmental relationships. There are various schools in the United States that teach and train chiropractors. To find one in your area, either look in your yellow pages under Chiropractic; ask at your local health food store, ask a friend who goes to one, ask your local chamber or go online to www.ChiroWeb.com. Also check the links listed below for the three largest chiropractic schools in the United States – Life University, Palmer College and Sherman Straight Chiropractic School.

Colon Hydrotherapy is a gentle purified water washing of the large intestine. The client lies on a massage table and with a colon hydrotherapy machine water is run very slowly into the colon. When slight pressure builds up in the colon, the water is released. The physical goals of each session are to hydrate the system, remove waste, stimulate peristalsis, rehabilitate the nerves, muscles, glands, circulatory and immune systems that form the components of the digestive system, and to reposition the intestines. A single colonic treatment is said to be equivalent to several enemas in removing toxic debris from the colon.

Craniosacral Therapy is a gentle, hands-on method of evaluating and enhancing the functioning of a physiological body system called the craniosacral system — comprised of the membranes and cerebrospinal fluid that surround and protect the brain and spinal cord. Using a soft touch generally no greater than five grams or about the weight of a nickel, practitioners release restrictions in the craniosacral system to improve the functioning of the central nervous system.

By complementing the body's natural healing processes, craniosacral therapy is increasingly used as a preventive health measure for its ability to bolster resistance to disease and is effective for a wide range of medical problems associated with pain and dysfunction, including:

- Migraine Headaches
- Chronic Neck and Back Pain

- ෬ Motor-Coordination Impairments
- ෬ Colic
- ෬ Autism
- ෬ Central Nervous System Disorders
- ෬ Orthopedic Problems
- ෬ Traumatic Brain and Spinal Cord Injuries
- ෬ Scoliosis
- ෬ Infantile Disorders
- ෬ Learning Disabilities
- ෬ Chronic Fatigue
- ෬ Emotional Difficulties
- ෬ Stress and Tension-Related Problems
- ෬ Fibromyalgia and other Connective-Tissue Disorders
- ෬ Temporomandibular Joint Syndrome (TMJ)
- ෬ Neurovascular or Immune Disorders
- ෬ Post-Traumatic Stress Disorder
- ෬ Post-Surgical Dysfunction

Ear Candling is an ancient technique of using a long, hollow pure beeswax and cotton candle to draw earwax, toxins, and moisture out of the ear. One end is placed in the external ear, the other end is lit. Ear candling is a safe, relaxing, and effective treatment for ear, sinus, and throat ailments.

Flower Essence is intended to alleviate negative emotional states that may contribute to illness or hinder personal growth. They help to give clarity to one's life but also give the courage, strength and commitment to follow and pursue one's goals and dreams. They help to develop a higher level of intuition, self-esteem, spirituality, creativity, and fun. The more the Essences are used, the more one is likely to experience greater awareness and happiness in one's life. Then everyone benefits: the individual, society and the planet. The effect of these Essences is similar to that of meditation in that they enable the person to access the wisdom of their Higher Self. This releases the negative beliefs held in the subconscious mind and allows the positive virtues of the Higher Self, including love, joy, faith, and courage to flood their being. When this happens the negative beliefs and thoughts are dissolved, balance is restored, and true healing occurs. Dr. Edward Bach discovered this healing method some 60 years ago, through the use of English flowering plants. He found 38 flowers to cover all known negative states of mind from which mankind can suffer, categorizing them in seven headings:

- ࢠ For anxiety and apprehension
- ࢠ For uncertainty and indecision
- ࢠ For loneliness
- ࢠ For insufficient interest in present circumstances
- ࢠ For over-sensitiveness to ideas and influence
- ࢠ For despondency and despair
- ࢠ For over-care for the welfare of others

Homeopathy is a complete system of medicine, which has been in worldwide use for nearly two hundred years. People suffering from all kinds of illnesses, from depression to arthritis, migraine to ulcers, and now the more "modern" illnesses, such as AIDS and ME, can be helped by homeopathy to regain health. Good homeopathy will not just drive away the symptoms but help the patient deal with the cause of the illness and regain good health.

Iridology is a quick, accurate, non-invasive, safe, and painless system of health analysis through the examination of the colored part of the eye known as the iris. The greatest feature and main advantage of Iridology over other forms of health screening is that changes appear in the iris before the physical symptom develops and therefore preventive action may be taken to improve health and avoid diseases, which might otherwise follow.

Magnetic field therapy or bio-magnetic therapy involves the use of magnets, magnetic devices, or magnetic fields to treat a variety of physical and emotional conditions, including circulatory problems, certain forms of arthritis, chronic pain, sleep disorders, and stress.

Naturopathy and the foundation of Naturopathic medicine is the philosophy of the "healing power of nature." This means that within every human organism there is a healing energy, which includes our immune system in the fuller sense of both the physical and the psyche, which is responsible for our wellness and our ability to heal and maintain health. Following this, the therapies are used to support and stimulate this healing power of nature must be in "the gentlest, least invasive, most efficient manner possible." The third Naturopathic premise is "to diagnose and treat the cause." Naturopaths do not simply treat the manifestation of the disease but rather search for the cause and treat it. To accomplish these goals, Naturopathic medicine incorporates many therapeutic modalities, such as herbal medicine, homeopathy, nutrition, hydrotherapy, food, exercise therapy, physical therapy, and manipulation of the bony and soft tissues, lifestyle, and counseling. Naturopaths are only recognized in a few states as licensed physicians, but their presence is growing every year.

Nutritional Counseling. Your diet is the foundation for good health and optimal healing. Finding a well-rounded, balanced diet for your personal body is the focus here. Dietitians and nutritionists help plan food and nutrition programs, and supervise the preparation and serving of meals. They can help prevent and treat illnesses by promoting healthy eating habits and suggesting diet modifications, such as less salt for those with high blood pressure or reduced fat and sugar intake for those who are overweight.

Reflexology is an ancient healing art using massage therapy on particular areas of the hands and feet. It is believed that each part of the body is intertwined through the nervous system to special points on the hands and feet. The science of reflexology stresses massaging particular areas of the hands and feet to bring mental, emotional, and physical health and well-being in the whole body. Pressure to certain points aids the body to heal itself.

Our bodies have the ability to heal itself. Following an injury, illness, and stress, our bodies become imbalanced. Stress alone is involved in over 80 percent of all illness. Reflexology can help the body to return to its natural balance. This gentle art of reflexology encourages the body to heal itself at its own pace. Reflexology treats the whole person so most people benefit from treatment. How does reflexology work? It is really quite simple. Pressing a reflex point on the foot or hand, a message is sent to a body part. That body part begins to let go of excess stress, tension, and congestion. Blood flows in, waste products are removed, circulation is normalized. The body begins to heal itself: a headache begins to disappear, fatigue turns to energy, back pain melts away, a fussy baby settles down, sinuses drain, hiccups stop, a hyperactive child or wakeful adult sleeps, and stress drains from the body. Reflexology is suitable for all ages. Reflexologists use their hands to gently apply pressure to the hands and feet concentrating on tender spots. The reflexologist can detect tiny imbalances in the hands and feet. When working on these points they release blockages and clear the pathways of energy flow to the body. Sensitive, trained hands can detect tiny deposits and imbalances in the feet and by working on these points, the reflexologist can release blockages and restore the free flow of energy to the whole body. Tensions are eased, and circulation and elimination is improved. This gentle therapy encourages the body to heal itself at its own pace, often counteracting a lifetime of misuse. Every body from the body of a newborn baby to the body of a centenarian can benefit from the relaxing and healing effects of reflexology. Reflexology applied to the feet or hands can help remove excess body tension, improve circulation, and normalize body function.

When properly applied, reflexology feels great and leaves a body feeling relaxed, renewed, and full of vitality. Reflexology not only positively affects our physical bodies, but also has a positive balancing effect on the mental, emotional, and spiritual parts of ourselves. Reflexology is easy to learn and can be applied by virtually any person eager enough to learn. Reflexology is an ancient healing technique that can help renew our mind and body. It is a safe and natural therapy used to harmonize the body and its healing abilities. It can help the individual to relax and restore the body's own balance.

To practice reflexology on yourself, purchase a reflexology chart, which is available in health food stores. Using the chart and your fingers, locate your reflex points in the hands or feet. Press on the reflexology point three times for ten seconds each time. When you have reached the right spot, it usually feels tender. The amount of tenderness on the hands or feet normally indicates the size of blockage. Do the pressure treatment for twenty to thirty minute sessions at a time, for two to three times a week. Some people experience frequent bowel movements in the first twenty-four hours after a reflexology treatment. This is the body's way of eliminating wastes and toxins.

Rolfing uses deep manipulation of the fascia to restore the body's natural alignment, which may have become rigid through injury, emotional trauma, and inefficient movement habits. The process, developed by biochemist Ida P. Rolf, involves ten sessions, each focusing on a different part of the body. It is a great therapy to have done on your body; it helps release lots of old memories, traumas, and pains.

Sound Therapy. A diagnostic and therapeutic technique used in sound healing. Sound healers read a patient's body by singing a series of tones and listening for imbalances in the natural frequencies of the body or its energy fields. Imbalances are said to be indicated by changes in the tone of the healer's voice. To correct a problem, the sound healer applies sound to the patient's body by singing certain tones near the affected organ or by applying tuning forks or electronic vibratory instruments to the body.

Water Therapy (also called pool therapy, hydrotherapy, or aquatic therapy) consists of a variety of aquatic-based treatments that are designed for back pain relief, to condition and strengthen muscles, and increase range of motion in the spine and other affected parts of the body. A water therapy exercise program can be used alone or in conjunction with other forms of physical therapy. The physical properties of water make it a highly desirable medium for treating back pain and other musculoskeletal injuries. Some of the most important properties are buoyancy, which help support the weight of the patient in a controlled environment. It promotes strengthening and conditioning of an injury, while reducing the risk of further injury due to loss of balance. Water therapy is fun and easy and a great way to get wet and gain from it!

Yoga is designed to integrate the body and mind connection, helping one to find their center. It originated in India more than 5,000 years ago. It was designed to help the body prepare for meditation. It helps relax ligaments and taunt muscles, reduces stress and tensions, and even improves flexibility. There are many forms of yoga.

- ∞ **Hatha Yoga** – utilizes different poses for the purpose of cleansing and strengthening the body, which focuses on a combination of breathing and postures.
- ∞ **Bikram Yoga** – done in a heated room of about 100 degrees to warm up your body. This form of yoga has a routine of 26 poses designed to work deeply into muscles and ligaments.
- ∞ **Kundalini Yoga** – focuses on releasing the kundalini energy. Kundalini refers to the serpent visualized as a snake coiled at the base of the spine. Through sound, breathing, and various postures, the kundalini is awakened and moves through the body.
- ∞ **Iyengar Yoga** – involves a precise focus on the physical alignment of the body. It is a form of Hatha where each pose is held for a longer period of time. Props are often used to make it easier to achieve the postures and the correct alignment of the body.

Yoga can either be done in the home using video tapes showing you the movements and explaining the breath work, or you can also take a class offered at various fitness centers and yoga centers. One should start out with a beginners program and gradually work into the style of yoga that is most comfortable. Yoga is extremely relaxing, burns calories, and can help improve muscle tone and flexibility. You move at your own pace and stretch only to the level that your body allows.

FEATURED WEBSITE LINKS:

- Acupuncture
  AcupunctureToday.com
- Associated Bodywork and Massage Professionals
  www.abmp.com
- American Massage Therapy Association
  www.amtamassage.org
- American Reflexology Certification Board
  www.arcb.net
- Chiropractic
  www.ChiroWeb.com
- The International Association for Colon Hydrotherapy
  www.i-act.org
- Craniosacral Therapy
  www.upledger.com
- International Iridology Practitioners Association
  www.iridologyassn.org
- Life University – College of Chiropractic
  www.lifewest.edu   1-800-788-4476
- Massage Information
  www.masssagetoday.com
- National Center for Complementary and Alternative Medicine
  www.nccam.nih.gov
- National Certification Board for Therapeutic Massage and Bodywork
  www.ncbtmb.com
- National Certification Commission for Acupuncture and Oriental Medicine
  www.nccaom.org
- Palmer College of Chiropractic (800)442-4476
  www.palmer.edu/PCC_Alumni/DCReferrals.htm
- The American Dietetic Association
  www.eatright.org
- Sherman Straight Chiropractic School
  www.sherman.edu

Chapter Thirteen

Inspiring Thoughts And Poems To Help Brighten Your Day

Positive thought is an important ingredient in the healing process. Whether we have positive or negative thoughts and energies in our lives, remains in our hands. A negative attitude adds strength to an illness and detracts from the power and healing abilities of the individual. Feeling bad or sorry for ourselves can actually shut down every system, in our body, including our immune system. On the other hand, feeling positive and good about ourselves can enhance the immune system, thereby affecting the overall quality of our lives. This is your life and there are no dress rehearsals!! No one's life is perfect, as much as the fairy tales and TV shows make us think they are. We all have illnesses, hard situations, difficult times, and losses to deal with. Have you noticed some people seem to handle their lives and situations better than others, and have you ever wondered why? A lot has to do with attitude! So I wrote this chapter to try to help you change your attitude towards yourself, your life, and your health.

So starting now, you are going to take an active role in your life, your health and your total well-being!! One step forward, no matter how small or slow is a movement in the right direction!! You are now an active participant and one step closer to total health and well-being !!

You are a WINNER ! What you think is what you become, so think positive and have a great life !

~Words To Live By~.....

DREAMS

"A dream is in the mind of the believer,
and in the hands of the doer"
"You are not given a dream,
without being given the power to make it come true."

FRIENDSHIP

"A friend is someone who walks in when the
rest of the world walks out."
"True friends are like diamonds, precious but rare."
"Don't walk in front of me, I may not follow."
"Don't walk behind me, I may not lead."
"Just walk beside me and be my friend."

GOD

"God sometimes puts us in the dark for us to see the light."
"God is able to do immeasurable deeds."
"Where God guides, He always provides."
"God's help is only a prayer away."
"God without man is still God. Man without God is nothing."
"Prayer changes things."

LOVE

"Love is never having to say you are sorry."
"When you love a person, you are giving him
the power to hurt you."
"Love is having to see more than what meets the eyes."
"You never lose by loving. You always lose by holding back."
"True love is like ghosts,
which everybody talks about and few have seen."

THE FUTURE
"Heal the past; live the present; dream the future."
"Do not start Today with the broken pieces of Yesterday."
"Destiny is not a matter of chance."
"It is a matter of choice: it is not a thing to be waited for,
it is a thing to be achieved."

LIFE
"Life will only come once, so make the most out of it."
"God didn't give us all things to enjoy life,
but life to enjoy all things."
"A journey of a thousand miles begins with a single step."
"Mistakes are not intended to down us,
rather they make us stronger."

RECIPE FOR A FAMILY PIE:
Add:
1 handful of FORGIVENESS
1 heaping cupful of LOVE
1 pound of UNSELFISHNESS
2 tablespoons of GOOD NATURE

Mix: Together with complete FAITH in GOD
Or UNIVERSAL LOVE
Then sprinkle Generously with THOUGHTFULNESS...
This makes a wonderful Family Pie....
Enjoy !!

RECIPE FOR A HAPPY CHILD

Add:
2 Teaspoons of CARE
1 Cup of KINDNESS
   2 Cups of SECURITY
2 Tablespoons of SAFETY
   1 Cup of LOVE
2 Cups of LOVING PARENTS
   1 Cup of RELIGION AND
   BELIEFS

Mix: Together with Care, Kindness, Security, Safety,
Love, Loving Parents, Religion and Beliefs.
KEEP HOT AT ALL TIMES,
NEVER LET GET WARM.
Mix thoroughly.
Bake forever.
Makes one happy child.

TO MAKE SUNSHINE:

Two equal parts of FAITH and KINDNESS,
   Add Enough LOVE for a suitable and even
   consistency.
    Blend in GENEROUSLY with
    THOUGHTFULNESS,
    Add ENCOURAGEMENT to taste.
A pinch of CHEERFULNESS will improve the
flavor.

Stir the whole thing with a hale and hearty
laugh,
   and share with everyone. It'll grow on you.
Too much love NEVER spoils children.
Children become spoiled when we substitute
"Presents" for "Presence."

SCRIPTURE CAKE
4 cups 1 Kings 4:22 (first part)
1 large Tbsp 1 Samuel 14:25
1 cup Judges 5:25 (last clause)
Season to taste of II Chronicles 9:9
2 cups Jeremiah 6:20
6 cups of Jeremiah 17:11
2 cups 1 Samuel 30:12
Pinch of Leviticus 2:13
2 cups Nahum 3:12 (found in the Apocrypha)
1/2 cup Genesis 24:20
1 Tbsp Number 17:8
2 Tsp Amos 4:5

Follow Solomon's advice for making good boys (Proverbs 23:14)
and you will have a good cake.

I ASKED THE LORD TO BLESS YOU
I asked the Lord to bless you
As I prayed for you today,
To guide you, and protect you
As you go along your way...

His / Her love is always with you
His / Her promises are true,
And when we give Him / Her all our cares
You know He / She will see us through.

So when the road you're traveling on
Seems difficult at best...
Just remember I'm here praying
And God will do the rest.

This world can never have too many blessings.
Do what you can, for who you
Can, with what you have, and
Where you are......

DON'T LOOK BACK
As you travel through life there are always those times
When decisions just have to be made,
When the choices are hard and solutions seem scarce
And the rain seems to soak your parade!

There are some situations where all you can
Do is to simply let go and move on,
Gather courage together and choose a direction
That carries you toward a new dawn.

So pack up your troubles and take a step forward.
The process of change can be tough.
But think about all the excitement ahead,
If you can be stalwart enough!
There could be adventures you never imagined
Just waiting around the next bend;
And wishes and dreams just about to come true
In ways you can't yet comprehend!

Perhaps you'll find friendships that spring from new interests,
As you challenge your status quo
And learn there are so many options in life
And so many ways you can grow!

Perhaps you'll go places you never expected
And see things that you've never seen,
Or travel to fabulous, faraway worlds and
Wonderful spots in between!

Perhaps you'll find warmth, affection and caring,
A "somebody special" who's there
To help you stay centered and listen with interest
to stories and feelings you share.

Perhaps you'll find comfort in knowing your friends
Are supportive of all that you do

And believe that whatever decisions you make;
They'll be the right choices for you!

So keep putting one foot in front of the other
And taking your life day by day.
There's a brighter tomorrow that's just down the road.
Don't look back, you're not going that way!

ALWAYS HAVE A DREAM
By Amanda Bradley

Forget about the days when it's been cloudy,
but don't forget your hours in the sun.
Forget about the times you've been defeated,
but don't forget the victories you've won.
Forget about mistakes that you can't change now
but don't forget the lessons that you've learnt.
Forget about misfortunes you encounter,
but don't forget the times your luck has turned.
Forget about the days when you've been lonely,
but don't forget the friendly smiles you've seen.
Forget about the plans that didn't seem to work out right,
but don't forget to always have a dream.

MASTERCARD

"There are some things money can't buy,
for everything else there's Master Card."
I'm sure you've all seen those commercials on TV.
Well, I'm not unlike those agencies promoting
their favorite credit card.
However, I'm here to advertise a different card.
You see, my life is a commercial for others to see.
I'm a card carrying representative for the Master's Card.
That's right, the MASTER'S CARD.

Let me tell you about it.
There are no finance charges, no payments due.
My bill has already been covered...it's a prepaid deal.
I couldn't afford the price, so Jesus stepped in and paid it for me.
My Name is written on the card for all to see.
It is accessible twenty-four hours a day from anywhere in the world.
The MASTER'S CARD has so many benefits
it's hard to list them all.
Let me share some of them with you...
you might want to apply for a personal card yourself.
Just for starters there is UNLIMITED GRACE.

That's right, there is no preset limit to the amount of grace you re-
ceive from the MASTER'S CARD.
Have you been looking for love in all the wrong places?
Then, look no farther than the MASTER'S CARD.
It offers the greatest rate on love that has ever been offered.
The MASTER'S CARD gives you access to many
"members only" benefits.
Want real joy despite the difficulties of life?
Apply for the MASTER'S CARD.
Want a lasting peace? Apply for the MASTER'S CARD.
Looking for something you can always rely on in a jam?
The MASTER'S CARD is perfect for you.

Another great thing about the MASTER'S CARD
is that it never expires.
Once you're a member, you're a member for life —
eternal life, that is.
Membership has its privileges, you know.
[Note: this membership is only revoked should you
choose another master.]

How do you receive the MASTER'S CARD?
Dial 1-800-ROMANS-10:9,
"If thou shalt confess with thy mouth the Lord Jesus, and shalt be-
lieve in thine heart that God hath raised him from the dead, thou
shalt be saved.
Jesus is standing by right now to take your call. Don't delay.
This a great offer won't last forever.
Peace, joy, and hope: Invaluable.
Faith, contentment, and assurance: Inestimable.
Salvation: Priceless.
Christian, yes, there are some things money can buy.
But for those other jewels of life there's the MASTER'S CARD.
Why not be an advertisement for the MASTER'S CARD?
Let your life be a commercial today for Jesus Christ.

HEALED AND WHOLE
By Carol Parrott

One day I dug a little hole
And put my hurt inside
I thought that I could just forget
I'd put it there to hide.

But that little hurt began to grow
I covered it every day
I couldn't leave it and go on
It seemed the price I had to pay.

My joy was gone, my heart was sad
Pain was all I knew.
My wounded soul enveloped me
Loving seemed too hard to do.

One day, while standing by my hole
I cried to God above
And said, "If You are really there --
They say, You're a God of Love!"

And just like that — He was right there
And just put His arms around me
He wiped my tears, His hurting child
There was no safer place to be.

I told Him all about my hurt
I opened up my heart
He listened to each and every word
To every sordid part.

I dug down deep and got my hurt
I brushed the dirt away
And placed it in the Master's hand
And healing came that day.
He took the blackness of my soul

And set my spirit FREE!
Something beautiful began to grow
Where the hurt used to be.

And when I look at what has grown
Out of my tears and pain
I remember every day to give my hurts to Him
And never bury them again.

LET GO AND LET GOD

As children bring their broken toys,
with tears for us to mend,
I brought my broken dreams to God,
because He is my friend.
But then instead of leaving Him
in peace to work alone,
I hung around and tried to help
with ways that were my own.
At last, I snatched them back again and cried,
"How can you be so slow?"
" My child," He said, "What could I do?
You never did let go."
"How can you be so slow?"
" My child," He said, "What could I do?
You never did let go."

"Ask and it shall be given to you;
Seek and you shall find;
Knock and the door shall be opened to you."

TO RISK
By Leo Buscalia

To laugh is to risk being a fool.
To weep is to risk appearing sentimental.
To reach out to another is to risk involvement.
To express feelings is to risk exposing your true self.
To place your ideas, your dreams, before the crowd
is to risk their loss.
To love is to risk not being loved in return.
To live is to risk dying.
To hope is to risk despair.
To try is to risk failure.
The person who risks nothing, does nothing, has nothing
and is nothing.
They may avoid suffering and sorrow,
But they simply cannot learn, feel, change, grow, love, or live.
Risks must be taken because, the greatest hazard in life is to risk
nothing. Only a person who risks is free.

PRAYER
May today there be peace within.
May you trust your highest power
that you are exactly where you are meant to be....
May you not forget the infinite possibilities
that are born of faith.
May you use those gifts that you have received, and
pass on the love that has been given to you....
May you be content knowing you are a child of God
and the Divine...
Let this presence settle into our bones, and
allow your soul the freedom to sing, dance, praise and love.
It is there for each and every one of you....

LIFE PHILOSOPHY

The most destructive habit.. Worry
The greatest joy...Giving
The greatest loss..Self-respect
The most satisfying work.............................Helping others
The ugliest personality trait ....Selfishness
The most endangered species................. Dedicated leaders
Our greatest natural resource...........................Our youth
The greatest "shot in the arm" ....Encouragement
The greatest problem to overcome .... Fear
The most effective sleeping pill ....Peace of mind
The most crippling disease...Excuses
The most powerful force in life. ....Love
The most dangerous outcast .... A gossiper
The world's most incredible computer .... The brain
The worst thing to be without...................................Hope
The deadliest weapon to a soul .... Our tongue
The two most power-filled words.........................."I CAN!"
The greatest asset.. Faith
The most worthless emotion....................................Self-pity
The most beautiful attire.. A smile
The most prized possession ....Integrity
The most powerful channel of communication.........Prayer
The most contagious spirit. .... Enthusiasm

LIFETIME RESOLUTIONS

Give up complaining............................... focus on gratitude
Give up pessimism ....become an optimist
Give up harsh judgments....................Think kind thoughts
Give up worry.................................... trust divine providence
Give up discouragement............................. be full of hope
Give up bitterness .... turn to forgiveness
Give up hatred....................................return good for evil
Give up negativism. ....be positive
Give up anger.. practice patience
Give up pettiness...put on maturity
Give up gloom................... enjoy the beauty All around you
Give up jealousy...pray for trust
Give up gossiping............................... control your tongue

TO REALIZE

To realize the value of ten years ... Ask a newly divorced couple.

To realize the value of four years ... Ask a graduate.

To realize the value of one year ...
Ask a student who has failed his final exam.

To realize the value of nine months ...
Ask a mother who gave birth to a still born.

To realize the value of one month ...
Ask a mother who has given birth to a premature baby.

To realize the value of one week ...
Ask an editor of a weekly newspaper.

To realize the value of one hour ...
Ask the lovers who are waiting to meet.

To realize the value of one minute ...
Ask a person who has missed teh train, bus or plane.

To realize the value of one second ...
Ask a person who has survived an accident.

To realize the value of one millisecond ...
Ask the person who has won a silver medal in the Olympics.

Time waits for no one. Treasure every moment you have. You will
treasure it even more when you can share it with someone special.

To realize the value of a friend ... Lose one.
This last one gives us ALL a reality check !!

NATURAL HIGHS - MAKE YOU FEEL GOOD

1   Falling in love
2. Laughing so hard your face hurts
3. A hot shower
4. No lines at the supermarket
5. A special glance
6. Getting mail
7. Taking a drive on a pretty road
8. Hearing your favorite song on the radio
9. Lying in bed listening to the rain outside
10. Hot towels fresh out of the dryer
11. Finding the sweater you want is on sale for half price
12. Chocolate milkshake (or vanilla!) (or strawberry!)
13. A long distance phone call
14. A bubble bath
15. Giggling
16. A good conversation
17. The beach
18. Finding a 20 dollar bill in your coat from last winter
19. Laughing at yourself
20. Midnight phone calls that last for hours
21. Running through sprinklers
22. Laughing for absolutely no reason at all
23. Having someone tell you that you're beautiful
24. Laughing at an inside joke
25. Friends
26. Accidentally overhearing someone say something nice about you
27. Waking up and realizing you still have a few hours left to sleep
28. Your first kiss (either the very first or with a new partner)
29. Making new friends or spending time with old ones
30. Playing with a new puppy
31. Having someone play with your hair
32. Sweet dreams
33. Hot chocolate
34. Road trips with friends

35. Swinging on swings
36. Wrapping presents under the Christmas tree while eating cookies and drinking your favorite tipple
37. Song lyrics printed inside your new CD so you can sing along without feeling stupid
38. Going to a really good concert
39. Making eye contact with a cute stranger
40. Winning a really competitive game
41. Making chocolate chip cookies
42. Having your friends send you homemade cookies
43. Spending time with close friends
44. Seeing smiles and hearing laughter from your friends
45. Holding hands with someone you care about
46. Running into an old friend and realizing that some things (good or bad) never change
47. Riding the best roller coasters over and over
48. Watching the expression on someone's face as they open a much desired present from you
49. Watching the sunrise
50. Getting out of bed every morning and being grateful for another beautiful day

So what have you done lately to help yourself feel good ?
Try some, you might like them !

I BELIEVE

I believe — that we don't have to change friends if we understand that friends change.

I believe — that no matter how good a friend is, they're going to hurt you every once in a while, and you must forgive them for that.

I believe — that true friendship continues to grow, even over the longest distance. Same goes for true love.

I believe — that you can do something in an instant that will give you heartache for life.

I believe —that it's taking me a long time to become the person I want to be.

I believe — that you should always leave loved ones with loving words. It may be the last time you see them.

I believe — that you can keep going long after you can't.

I believe —that we are responsible for what we do, no matter how we feel.

I believe — that either you control your attitude or it controls you.

I believe — that regardless of how hot and steamy a relationship is at first, the passion fades and there had better be something else to take its place.

I believe — that heroes are the people who do what has to be done, when it needs to be done, regardless of the consequences.

I believe — that money is a lousy way of keeping score.

I believe — that my best friend and I can do anything or nothing and have the best time.

I believe — that sometimes the people you expect to kick you when you're down, will be the ones to help you get back up.

I believe — that sometimes when I'm angry, I have the right to be angry, but that doesn't give me the right to be cruel.

I believe — that just because someone doesn't love you the way you want them to, doesn't mean they don't love you with all they have.

I believe — that maturity has more to do with what types of experiences you've had and what you've learned from them, and less to do with how many birthdays you've celebrated.

I believe — that it isn't always enough to be forgiven by others. Sometimes you have to learn to forgive yourself.

I believe — that no matter how bad your heart is broken the world doesn't stop for your grief.

I believe — that our background and circumstances may have influenced who we are, but we are responsible for who we become.

I believe — that just because two people argue, it doesn't mean they don't love each other. And just because they don't argue, it doesn't mean they do.

I believe — that you shouldn't be so eager to find out a secret. It could change your life forever.

I believe — that two people can look at the exact same thing and see something totally different.

I believe — that your life can be changed in a matter of hours by people who don't even know you.

I believe — that even when you think you have no more to give, when a friend cries out to you, you will find the strength to help.

I believe —that credentials on the wall do not make you a decent human being.

I believe — that the people you care about most in life are taken from you too soon.

EMERGENCY NUMBERS
Need some more advice...seek....

When in sorrow, call John 14
When men fail you, call Psalm 27
If you want to be fruitful, call John 15
When you have sinned, call Psalm 51
When you worry, call Matthew 6:19-34
When you are in danger, call Psalm 91
When God seems far away, call Psalm 139
When your faith needs stirring, call Hebrews 11
When you are lonely and fearful, call Psalm 23
When you grow bitter and critical, call 1 Corinthians 13
For Paul's secret to happiness, call Col. 3:12-17
For idea of Christianity, call 2Corinthians 5:5-19
When you feel down and out, call Romans 8:1-30
When you leave home for labor or travel, call Psalm 121
When your prayers grow narrow or selfish, call Psalm 67
For a great invention/opportunity, call Isaiah 55
When you want courage for a task, call Joshua 1
How to get along with fellow men, call Roman 12
When you think of investments/returns, call Mark 10
If you are depressed, call Psalm 27
If your pocketbook is empty, call Psalm 37

There are two ways to live your life.
One is as though nothing is a miracle.
The other is as though everything is a miracle.
Albert Einstein (1879-1955)

HELLO THERE, NICE PERSON

Hello There, Nice Person Did Anyone Ever Tell You,
Just How Special You Are?
The Light That You Emit Might Even Light A Star.

Did Anyone Ever Tell You
How Important You Make Others Feel?
Somebody Out Here Is Smiling
About Love That Is So Real

Did Anyone Ever Tell You How Many Times,
When They Were Sad, Your E-mail Or Phone Calls
Made Them Smile A Bit, In Fact It Made Them Glad?

For the Time You Spend Sending Things And Sharing
Whatever You Find There Are No Words To Thank You,
But Somebody, Thinks You're Fine

Did Anyone Ever Tell You Just How Much They Like You?
Well, My Dearest Friend, Today I Am Telling You
I Believe That Without A Friend You Are Missing Out On A Lot!!!
Don't Be Confused By Friends And Acquaintances,
There Is A Difference!
Have A Nice Day, And I'm Glad We Are Friends!!!

REASON, SEASON, AND LIFETIME

People come into your life for a reason, a season, or a lifetime.
When you figure out which it is, you know exactly what to do.

When someone is in your life for a **REASON**, it is usually to meet
a need you have expressed outwardly or inwardly. They have come
to assist you through a difficulty, to provide you with guidance and
support, to aid you physically, emotionally, or spiritually.

They may seem like a godsend, and they are. They are there for
the reason you need them to be.Then, without any wrong doing on
your part or at an inconvenient time, this person will say or do something to bring the relationship to an end. Sometimes they die. Sometimes they walk away. Sometimes they act up or out and force you to
take a stand.

What we must realize is that our need has been met, our desire
fulfilled; their work is done. The prayer you sent up has been
answered, and it is now time to move on.

When people come into your life for a **SEASON**, it is because
your turn has come to share, grow, or learn. They may bring you an
experience of peace or make you laugh. They may teach you something you have never done. They usually give you an unbelievable
amount of joy. Believe it! It is real!
But, only for a season.

LIFETIME relationships teach you lifetime lessons —those things
you must build upon in order to have a solid emotional foundation.
Your job is to accept the lesson, love the person or people (anyway)
and put what you have learned to use in all other relationships and
areas of your life. It is said that love is blind,
but friendship is clairvoyant.

Thank you for being a part of my life...

ONLY IF WE BELIEVE

To believe is to know that
every day is a new beginning.
It is to trust that miracles do happen,
and dreams really do come true.

To believe is to see angels
dancing among the clouds,
to know the wonder of a stardust sky
and the wisdom of the man in the moon.

To believe is to know the value
of a nurturing heart, and
the beauty of an aging hand,
for it is through their teachings we learn to love.

To believe is to find the strength and
courage that lies within us
when it is time to pick up
the pieces and begin again.

To believe is to know we are not alone,
that life is a gift and
this is our time to cherish it
with all our heart and soul.

To believe is to know that wonderful
surprises are just waiting to happen,
And all our hopes and dreams
are within reach ... only if we believe.

Author Unknown

A FIFTH GRADER'S POINT OF VIEW ON HOW GOD IS IN OUR TV AND EVERYWHERE IN OUR LIVES

BAYER ASPIRIN	He works miracles.
FORD	He's got a better idea.
COKE	He's the real thing.
HALLMARK CARDS	He cares enough to send His very best.
TIDE	He gets the stains out that others leave behind.
GENERAL ELECTRIC	He brings good things to life.
SEARS	He has everything.
ALKA-SELTZER	Try him, you'll like Him.
SCOTCH TAPE	You can't see him, but you know He's there.
DELTA	He's ready when you are.
ALLSTATE	You're in good hands with Him.
VO-5 HAIR SPRAY	He holds through all kinds of weather.
DIAL SOAP	Aren't you glad you have Him. Don't you wish everybody did.
THE U.S. POST OFFICE	Neither rain, nor snow, nor sleet nor ice will keep Him from His appointed destination.

~REMEMBER~

If God had a refrigerator, your picture would be on it.
If He/She had a wallet, your photo would be in it.
He/She sends you flowers every spring.
He/She sends you a sunrise every morning.
Whenever you want to talk, He/She listens.
He/She can live anywhere in the universe,
Yet He/She chooses your heart.
Face it, friend, He/She is crazy about you!

YOUR INSPIRATION: LET ME SIMPLY BE YOUR FRIEND

I'd like to capture a rainbow and stick it in a big box so that
anytime you wanted to, you could reach in
and pull out a piece of sunshine.

I'd like to build you a mountain that you could call your very own
a place to find serenity in those times
when you feel the need to be
closer to yourself.

I'd like to be the one who's there when you're lonely or troubled,
or you just need someone to hold on to.

I'd like to do all this and more
to make your life happy.

But, sometimes, it isn't easy to do the things I would like to do
or give the things I would like to give.
So... until I learn how to
catch rainbows and build mountains,
let me do for you which I know best...

Let me simply be your friend.

BEGINNING TODAY

Beginning today I will no longer worry about yesterday.
It is in the past and the past will never change.
Only I can change by choosing to do so.

Beginning today I will no longer worry about tomorrow.
Tomorrow will always be there, waiting for me to
make the most of it.
But I cannot make the most of tomorrow without first
making the most of today.

Beginning today I will look in the mirror and
I will see a person worthy of my respect and admiration.
This capable person looking back at me is someone
I enjoy spending time with and someone I would
like to get to know better.

Beginning today I will cherish each moment of my life.
I value this gift bestowed upon me in this world and
I will unselfishly share this gift with others.
I will use this gift to enhance the lives of others.

Beginning today I will take a moment to step off the beaten path and
to revel in the mysteries I encounter.
I will face challenges with courage and determination.
I will overcome what barriers there may be
which hinder my quest for growth and self-improvement.

Beginning today I will take life one day at a time, one step at a time.
Discouragement will not be allowed to taint my positive self-image,
my desire to succeed or my capacity to love.

Beginning today I walk with renewed faith in human kindness.
Regardless of what has gone before,
I believe there is hope for a brighter and better future.

Beginning today I will open my mind and my heart.
I will welcome new experiences. I will meet new people.
I will not expect perfection from myself or anyone else,
perfection does not exist in an imperfect world.
But I will applaud the attempt to overcome human foibles.

Beginning today I am responsible for my own happiness and
I will do things that make me happy . . .
admire the beautiful wonders of nature,
listen to my favorite music,
pet a kitten or a puppy,
soak in a bubble bath . . .
pleasure can be found in the most simple of gestures.

Beginning today I will learn something new;
I will try something different;
I will savor all the various flavors life has to offer.
I will change what I can and the rest I will let go.
I will strive to become the best me I can possibly be.

Beginning today. And every day.

Just a thought, but as I often think of you and
realize how much God loves you,
sometimes I think we need to also love ourselves through His eyes.

God Bless.

I hope these inspirational poems, prayers and sayings help you find good in your day. Is the glass half full or half empty, it's your decision and your attitude that answers that question! Remember attitudes are contagious, is yours worth catching?

Chapter Fourteen

CONCLUSION

how Me, Teach Me, Heal Me, a Beginner's Guide to Natural An-
swers, was written to help you get better control of your life and
your health, and to give you new and natural answers to health
problems and concerns, and to teach you that your health is your responsibility, not anyone else's, doctors included! Personal health and
well-being are an individual's responsibility. Optimal health doesn't
"just happen;" it takes time, commitment, and work. Wellness means
practicing healthy lifestyle behaviors that will enhance your well-being
while decreasing your risk of disease. A wellness lifestyle encompasses
several dimensions. These dimensions include physical, mental, emotional, spiritual and environmental factors.

I hope I have given you some new tools and techniques to start on
your road to total health and well-being. This book is meant to be a
guide to everyone, whether you are fighting a major illness or dis-ease
or you are just having a bad day and a sore throat. My goal was to answer some of those questions stated in Chapter One such as: Where
do I start? What is it about? How do I know what to do? What are my
friends talking about? Will it hurt me? What other options do I have?
The doctors are giving up on me now what? How do I find someone to
help me along my path to getting well? This book is meant to inspire

and motivate you by giving you the strength to keep going and finding new answers and hope for your own life.

As you become aware of your physical, emotional, mental and spiritual condition, you can act quickly to prevent illness and disease, if you are out balance. I hope you have learned from this book and found many different opportunities to embrace for your total health and well-being. This is your life and there are no dress rehearsals!!

Medicine has its place in society, and I thank the medical field for the advancement and technology that allowed my surgery. However, I do believe GOD didn't make junk, and we don't need all those drugs and surgeries! I think we can heal and cure our bodies naturally, if we just have the resources and tools available to us. I want to help empower the people of today to make a difference in their lives tomorrow. I want to share my futuristic dream with you, as one day I hope we meet in person.

My current dream is to build an *all-inclusive holistic center named New Horizons New Visions Health and Well-Being Center*. People would be able to find the best natural practioneers and answers to their health problems under one roof in this center. You would be able to get a massage, a chiropractic adjustment, an acupuncture treatment, a reflexology treatment, rolfing, cranial sacral work, and many others types of natural treatments to help enhance your total body, all of which I have experienced personally along my path to healing. Also available in this treatment center would be a psychic readings, numerology readings, astrology charts, yoga, meditation classes, tai chi, water aerobics, color therapy and many, many more alternative techniques!!

New Horizons New Visions Health And Well-Being Center represents one of the most important projects in America for centers dedicated to human development. Because of its structural characteristics and location, as well as its spirit, *New Horizons New Visions Health And Well-Being Center* offers the ideal space and conditions for the development of the whole human being. Our goal is a life in balance, with spiritual and physical freshness, youth, freedom, and harmony. This goal is worth pursuing. Health is the basic element that we need to be able to make the most of all the freedoms that our world can offer.

NEW HORIZONS NEW VISIONS HEALTH AND WELL-BEING CENTER MISSION STATEMENT:

We at *New Horizons New Visions Health and Well-Being Center* are committed to show, teach, and help each individual in a safe and caring environment, creating a life style to achieve an overall state of health and well-being on all levels of the mind, body, and spirit.

We will be an all-inclusive holistic center that offers the best natural practitioners in each available field under one roof.

Our lifetime goal is to offer these services to anyone seeking them in the United States, and hopefully in a facility in your state, less than a day's drive away.

Structurally *New Horizons New Visions Health And Well-Being Center* will be a conglomerate of nine buildings shaped into an octagon layout containing a multi-purpose auditorium for artistic activities, large conference and seminar rooms; four Practitioners buildings for diverse natural therapies; a church with a chapel inside; a vegetarian restaurant; a bookstore with a juice bar, and a *Pamper Me* building for personal growth, including a fitness center, a sauna/steam room, a swimming pool, a hot tub, and meditation rooms. Adjacent to the complex will be two octagon complexes each with nine small cottages of either one or two bedrooms, providing living quarters for our overnight guests to use. Beautiful gardens, waterfalls, many angel and dolphins figurines, and a wonderful natural environment will encompass the center, making it a truly warm and caring natural home. The cozy atmosphere will invite you to rest, to breathe fresh air, to enjoy silence, find inner peace and happiness, and gaze at the wonderful surrounding views.

The complex and its buildings will be designed in the shape of an octagon, as this is considered perfect feng shui. The Chinese believe that the practice of Feng Shui will bring prosperity, health benefits, and well-being, and this is inline with our mission and purpose.

One of the main attractions of *New Horizons New Visions Health And Well-Being Center* is doubtlessly its *Pamper Me* building. Its state-of-the-art facilities will include a dynamic indoor pool, steam baths and saunas, hot tubs, a state-of-the-art fitness room, an exercise room for taking yoga, tai chi or other exercise classes, and several meditation rooms which allow you the quiet time to re-connect with your inner-self and peace of mind.

Another wonderful attraction will be the *New Horizons New Visions Health And Well-Being Center Vegetarian Restaurant*, able to cater up to 250 people, offering a high standard of international vegetarian cuisine ranging from Mediterranean, Japanese, and Italian to Mexican. Seating will be available both inside and on the patio for our guests dining pleasure. Eating at *New Horizons New Visions Health And Well-Being Center* will be a uniquely satisfying and enlightening experience. How can spa food taste so flavorful and rich, even sinful? The secret will lie in the use of organic meats and seafood, fresh indigenous herbs, and vegetables from our garden and the dishes, which will be created with great care and love, with special attention to the detail of service and quality. In addition, the restaurant will offer many other dietary menus, to cater for special circumstances, and given with professional advice. We will constantly renovate the tasting menu as well as the a la carte menu and fresh salad and fruit bar choices. Only the finest of natural, organically grown ingredients will be used in all of our dishes. The final result: satisfaction and delight.

The bookstore located in the center of the complex will be another star attraction to the complex. With its juice bar, music room, child's reading room and assortment of wonderful inspiring books, magazines, and crystals; this will be a place our guests can linger for hours. Local and national authors will be invited to visit, mingling among the guests.

Our practitioners' services will range from A to Z, including but not limited to, acupuncture, chiropractic, nutrition, reiki, and massage and everything in-between. We will be the most complete holistic center in the United States. We will house the best of the best in natural practitioners available here in the United States under one roof.

The multi-purpose building will encompass many activities such as national speakers, wedding receptions, workshops, and courses in yoga, tai chi, meditation, reiki, music, art, crystals, and color therapies. The administration offices will also be located in this building.

The church will be a non-denominational facility with the ability to seat up to 250 people, with live and surround sound music, projected TV screens and a raised stage area. A small intimate chapel and prayer room will be located inside the church building.

Beautifully landscaped gardens, each with a theme of their own, with numerous waterfalls and sitting benches among them will enhance the outside environment. The butterfly garden located next to the multi-purpose building, will embrace some of Mother Earth's wonderful creatures. The angel garden located next to the church will encompass many different styles of angels among the beautiful landscaping. The labyrinth garden will be home to a breathtaking labyrinth maze, and an open bonfire. The herbal garden located next to the restaurant will grow fresh organic herbs and vegetables, which will be used in our restaurant. The sea life garden will be comprised of various sea life creatures both on the ground and in statue form. The dolphin garden located next to the *Pamper Me* building will touch your inner child and you will want take you for a ride in the ocean, without getting wet! The water palace and crystal garden will be home to some of the world's most gorgeous crystals and minerals with which Mother Earth has ever graced us. The running waters will invite you to throw your lucky pennies in and make a wish for your dreams to come true. We leave the best for last. The *Child's Play Garden* is a place where you can be and act like a kid again. But be forewarned – our angels like to play in these gardens, too!

The paths connecting these wonderful gardens, waterfalls and buildings are called the *Steps to the Stars*. Contributors can have their dedication engraved into the octagon shaped stepping-stones, as a tribute to those who are special in their lives.

Our accommodations will be octagon in shape, featuring one and two bedroom suites, in a breathtaking setting. Each room will have a private patio, some with a panoramic view. The center building will accommodate the laundry facilities, and a community room with a spacious lounge, large terrace, breathtaking gardens, and a few select vending machines. This will allow our guests to intermingle with other guests and make new friends. Special touches, such as fresh flowers, and candles will make every moment at *New Horizons New Visions Health And Well-Being Center* a special one.

New Horizons New Visions Health And Well-Being Center is coming into being to offer its services and facilities to all those who are trying to find solutions to their health problems or who are wishing to improve their well-being naturally. Our first center will be located in Goodyear, Arizona, in one of the most peaceful areas of Arizona. Our second location will be in Port St. Lucie, Florida, a peaceful hometown city on the east coast of Florida. Our future goals include building a *New Horizons New Visions Health And Well-Being Center* in almost every state within a ten-year period. This will allow everyone new choices and alternatives to their health care and well-being.

Our society is overwhelmed by an excess of materialism and vertiginous pace, which cause feelings of fragmentation, confusion and pressure throughout our lives, both in our personal relationships and at work. Many people end up expressing their unbalanced condition through illness, sometimes severe, and then find conventional medicine limited to solve their problems. Without underestimating the contribution of conventional medicine to health care, *New Horizons New Visions Health And Well-Being Center* will offer a different approach, helping to alleviate ill health through treating the person as a whole combining all levels of being: physical, emotional, psychological, and energetic.

The spiritual soul of *New Horizons New Visions Health And Well-Being Center* enables the energetic, spiritual, and physical condition of the human being to develop. The philosophy of *New Horizons New Visions Health And Well-Being Center* is based upon the concept of the human being as a whole. From that whole vision, we believe that the human being has the capacity to transform, grow, and cure itself, once people get the means to really connect with themselves, with their inner being. People will come to one of our facilities for either days or weeks of indulgence, or they can just pop by for lunch, or for two or three hours after work.

When you walk onto the grounds, your head will be full of thoughts, soon to dissolve into the air. The need for silence, relaxation, harmony and an internal balance is becoming increasingly important in our daily lives. In order to guarantee absolute relaxation and to develop new ideas, a harmonic interaction of mind, body, and soul is essential. It is now your time to feel good and unwind. Wellness days must be simple.

So as you can see, I have big dreams and goals for this lifetime! If you are interested in knowing more about the holistic centers I am going to build or want to help me build them, please contact me. I wish you much love, light and happiness on your journey to health, happiness and total well-being!!

So starting now – you are going to take an active role in your life, your health and your total well-being!! One step forward, no matter how small or slow is a movement in the right direction. You are now an active participant and one step closer to total health and well-being. You are a WINNER!

"My angels have taught me so much about life, love, and laughter, and how to really enjoy the journey we all call "life," and now I am being guided to share that knowledge with you!!"

If I can help you in any way to finding your path to total health and happiness, please do not hestitate to contact me !!

I wish you all the health, happiness and well-being you deserve in one lifetime !!

MAY THE ANGELS BE WITH YOU EVERY STEP OF THE WAY !!

Contributors

CHAPTER FOUR

A special thank you to Susanne at Colour Energy Corporation for her contribution to this chapter.

COLOUR ENERGY CORPORATION
1682 West 75th Avenue
Vancouver, British Columbia V6P 6G2
Voice: 604-687-3757
FAX: 604-687-3758
Toll Free: 800- 225-1226
www.colourenergy.com
colour@colourenergy.com

CHAPTER FIVE:

A special thank you to Becky Blair and Rev. Karen Wilkinson for their contributions to the Crystal Chapter.

Becky Blair
4911 NW 29th Street
Gainesville, FL 32605
Voice: 352-222-6336
FAX: 352-336-5937
rocksandglassbb@yahoo.com

Rev Karen Wilkinson
3209 Port St Lucie Blvd # 134
Port St Lucie, FL 34953
Voice: 772-597-0717
FAX: 772-597-0718
Kwafty@adelphia.net

CHAPTER SIX

A special thank you to Rev. Karen Wilkinson for her contribution to the Candle Chapter.

Rev Karen Wilkinson
3209 Port St Lucie Blvd # 134
Port St Lucie, FL 34953
Voice: 772-597-0717
FAX: 772-597-0718
Kwafty@adelphia.net

CHAPTER EIGHT

A special thank you to Brian Dean for his contribution to the massage portion of this chapter.

Brian Dean
13245 Atlantic Blvd, Suite 4-216
Jacksonville, FL 32225
Voice: 904-534-3121
http://www.CaringPalms.com
Brian@CaringPalms.com

A special thank you to Rosann Lynch for her contribution to the raindrop therapy portion of this chapter.

Rosann Lynch, CMT / LST
716 Lighthouse Avenue, Suite F
Pacific Grove, Ca 93950
Voice: 831-646-9521
handz2000@aol.com

CHAPTER TEN

A special thank you to Nature's Sunshine and Viable Herbal Solutions for their contributions to this chapter.

Nature's Sunshine Products, Inc.
Corporate Headquarters
75 East 1700 South
Provo, Utah
Voice: 1-800-223-8225

Viable Herbal Solutions
P.O. Box 969
Morrisville, PA 19067-0969
1-800-505-9475

CHAPTER ELEVEN

A special thank you to Lanis Loveday Chidel for her contribution to the Feng Shui chapter.

Lanis Loveday Chidel
Artist/designer
Professional member of the International Feng Shui Guild.
LaPaChi Art & Design
5007 Melrow Ct
Tampa, Fl 33624
Voice: 813-961-9307
lapachi@aol.com

About the Author:

Acaysha, is an angelic name that means "Angel of Diversity and Strength." Today, Acaysha Dolfin, with the help of her band of seven angels, is A Miracle, An Angel and An Inspiration to many people in need, counseling them and giving them healings, hope, and motivation to keep on living, no matter how tough the going gets. She is a National Advocate for The Epilepsy Foundation of America and holds a Doctorate of Metaphysics degree. She is full-time author, motivational speaker and Reiki Master, who travels the country helping others heal through her life stories, survival experiences and warm angelic advice. She teaches them how to have their own band of angels in their life, so they can live their life to the fullest. Her story uplifts anyone who is trying to cope with an illness, disability, or is just down and out, discouraged or depressed. Her newest career goal is to build an "all inclusive holistic center" called *New Horizons New Visions Health and Well-Being Center*, where people can find the best natural practioneers under one roof and get natural answers to their health problems and concerns. Please feel free to contact her personally at:

Acaysha Dolfin
500 N Estrella Parkway, #B2-264
Goodyear, AZ 85338
623 594 1484
888 759 5371
http://www.acaysha.com
acaysha@gmail.com
acaysha@acaysha.com

New Horizons And My Angels
Guided Meditations, Books, Audio Book CDS - Order Form

Title	Description	Qty	Price	Ext Price
Swim With The Dolphins CD	Go swim with the dolphins, find a place and time to reenergize, and heal. Dolphins are the oldest and most powerful healers on the planet.		1- $13 2 - $25 3 - $33	
Field Of Angels CD	Come meet your own band of angels, as this guided meditation takes you on a journey to a beautiful garden, where the angels will be waiting for you		1- $13 2 - $25 3 - $33	
Angels In The Rainbow CD	This meditation takes you up into a rainbow, wraps you in the seven colors and allows you to go fly with your angels		1- $13 2 - $25 3 - $33	
New Horizons And My Angels Book	This inspiring true story of Acaysha's journey through brain surgery recovery, will bring you a ray of hope; a breath of renewal; a seed of faith; and a belief in miracles and angels		$22.00	
New Horizons And My Angels Audio CD	This is the audio portion of the book NEW HORIZONS AND MY ANGELS. Listen to Acaysha and her many angels, as the read the book to you and take you a fantastic healing journey		$29.95	
Show Me, Teach Me Heal Me, A Beginner's Guide To Natural Answers	This book is easy to read and understand. It is a great beginner's guide to the alternative and complementary health choices that are available today. It will help guide you down the path to health and well-being and teach you how to choose natural answers for your life.		$22.95	

Special Pricing: One Meditation CD $13, Two for $25,
Three for $33 (Shipping included   **Total Cost: $** _____

Name: _____

Phone: _____

Address: _____

City: _____   State: _____   Zip: _____

E-Mail: _____

To pay by credit card:

Name of Cardholder: _____

Credit Card Number: _____

3 digit security code _____

Expiration: _____Card Type: Visa _____ MasterCard _____

Make checks payable to NHMA. Mail this form to:
NHMA
500 N Estrella Parkway, #B2-264
Goodyear, AZ 85338